The Life

Journey of the Huddy's Let's go Back in Time

By

Susan Huddy Blais

Table of Contents

Overview of my life

This is my own story and remembrance of my young life starting with school days. Then married life, and children with the relatives that I remember and ones that I lost. As Paul Harvey would say "The rest of the story". In my own right mind and memory here is my own life story. I Tom Lee Huddy now 78 years of age, was born December 7th, 1931 to Thomas A. Huddy and his wife Nellie Etta (Campbell) Huddy around Haydenville Wolfe Basin near Nelsonville and Logan Ohio. I was the oldest son of the three of us boys and then came brother Robert (Bob) and after him came James R (Jim) the youngest of all of us. We had an older sister, Rona Eleanora Huddy and she was 12 years older than I. I was put into school at the age of five in 1936 at a school in Chauncey Dover, Ohio in first grade. Rona was put in 3rd grade at the age of seven there and it was 5 miles from the farm. Dad and mother lived on a large farm near the plains near Athens, Ohio in a small village of Beaumont, and the farm was owned by Sunday Creek Coal mining company. Grandpa L.D. Huddy leased it to farm and had my father and his brother moved into the large farmhouse with seventeen rooms in it at Beaumont, Ohio near the plains. My mother, Dow Jr, and Aunt Pauline would help L.D., their father, farm the land. L.D. Huddy's real name was Lorenzo Dow Huddy and his nickname was Doodle. He was 125 lbs., hard to work for and to get along with. To this day I don't see why Dad and Uncle Dow Jr ever stayed on to help him on that farm. Maybe because he handled the money, if any at the end of the great depression. Back in the Depression, I remember long lines of hungry people with boxes and crates for blocks to get food for their hungry families. They would receive rolled dried oats, dried prunes, bread, and some sort of hog-side pork salted. They would get peanut butter and raisins etc... It was hard times and our country was in real trouble then and we did live on a big farm our grandpa controlled. He was in control of everything like farm tools, horses, cattle, and tractors, and owned about everything so to speak. If Dad or Dow needed meat from the

1

smokehouse they had to ask L.D. for it to make a meal. They would work on harvest and he would put money in his pocket and pay Dad and Dow whatever he wanted to. As time went on L.D., Dad and Dow Jr. drank at every bar and joint in the county of Athens well known for fighting and fussing with each other over farm things and such. They would bring these fights home around us small ones and Uncle Dow Jr and Grandpa would fist fight and cut each other with corn knives and bring blood on each other. Grandpa Doodle didn't care much for us kids because we were too young to work and be used by him. He didn't like us to play in the big barns, and three of them were full of hay and bailed straw. We loved to make tunnels and crawl through them like caves. That was a lot of fun for us and would make him real mad at us, so, he would cuss at us. One morning I remember he had a hangover and we boys and Aunt Mildred's boys were fussing over something and Grandpa went into the shed, came out with a long buggy whip or bullwhip, and started on us. It hurt and stung and only Bob got away and ran through the garden to the house to tell about Grandpa to Mother and Aunt Mildred. The real fight was on. They disliked our little dogs and one of them took fits and just ran in circles and slobbered at the mouth. Uncle Dow just shot it and the other one knocked a dish or tray of doughnuts out of Bob's hands and our dad ran out of the barn, where they were working, and killed it. He killed it with a long piece of iron pipe right in front of us kids and man that was sad. Then off the three farmers went to spend the day drinking and stayed out until morning. Meanwhile, Pauline, Mildred, and the Mother fed the farm stock and milked the cows. We boys, along with Denny and Rudy, helped out the best we could at a very young age and size. We had a white-faced bull that was real mean and used for breeding our milk cows. This bull got out of the fence at the barn and we boys told our mothers. Aunt Pauline and they tried to get him back inside the fence but the bull smelled the blood of the dog Uncle Dow shot the day before and it went plain nuts and rooted and pawed the ground and ran after mother and our aunts. They got up on the hay wagon and it tried to upset the wagon. When Dad, Dow, and Grandpa came home, they put him back in the field. Then the three of them got into a fight because we children and our aunts didn't do the chores right. Okay, man get out of the drinking joints, and get back to the farm and do it the way you want. We had a pond where the livestock drank spring-fed water and the pond was full of sunfish, bluegills, and mud catfish and we loved to fish and hunt duck eggs. It had cat tails and swamps all around it and our ducklings would follow the mother duck out on the pond for their first lesson on swimming. Such fun just to watch them. The Hocking Valley Railroad was between the Hocking River and our farm. There were two trains, a freight, and a passenger train. The first time I rode a passenger train was when I went to the Athens County Fair with my mother, Pauline, my sister, and two brothers. In 1939 things on the Athens farm weren't doing well and Mother told Dad to make up his mind if we were moving out or if he was staying. She told him she was moving us children out from under his father L.D. Huddy because she had all she could take of him. My mom and dad separated over this and mom moved us to Haydenville with Charley and Mildred at a road called Laurel Run and we were put in school at Union Furnace. Rona was in the 5th grade now, I was in 3rd, Bob was in 2nd and Jim was in 1st. I sat at a table in a small chair. It was my 3rd-grade teacher's first year. She was a widow from Logan, Ohio, and her name was Marion Able. She was my teacher until 10th grade and she appointed me to be the class artist which included the Farmer's Institute (Which later was called FFA). She favored us and Mildred and Charlie's family. I ran errands, dusted erasers, and helped make Valentine boxes for the class. After a while, Dad's brothers Dow and Pauline broke up the farming with L.D. Huddy. Dad and mother got back together and they found this old run-down home at the crossroads at the top of Laurel Run big hill. I think they paid $800.00 for the house and five acres that were half-timber and half-cleared with a very nice deep well. The well never went dry and was always cold and good. At that time Dad didn't have a job to work at and at first it was rough. The home was an old log house that was ready to fall down and had no porch at all. Eventually, Dad got a full-time job at Haydenville Natco Tile and Brick Plant so little by little things started to get better for our family. Dad and I cut the back part of an old car off to make a small homemade pickup truck so he had a way to work and each evening he would bring home tile and bricks from the factory dump yard called Seconds. They would have maybe a chip on them or a small crack so they dumped them and they were free to anyone who worked at the plant. Well, Dad could haul a ton in the old homemade truck and we boys would unload and stack them at the house. I could drive our country roads and Bob, Jim and I would go to the river bridge and shovel river sand on Saturday because that is when the old truck was at home due to Dad having off most Saturdays. Dad let us haul river sand that belonged to Charley Price off his land and told Dad we could help ourselves. We had a homemade mesh screen that we would pitch the sand on, so the good sand would drop through the screen and other things wouldn't. We would have some nice river sand to mix our cement with for sidewalks and laying tile and bricks. Everything we ever did to our home came from hard labor for us, to make do. Then we also built a nice garage, later a barn, and then a hog pen. In time our place started to look like an old country home place. We didn't have electricity or a phone until about the time Dad and Mother sold the place. We lived at the crossroads while World War II was going on and at the top of Laurel Run Hill. I got my first gun at age 11 and it was a 16-gauge shotgun. I received my first hunting license in 1942 but because of World War II shells were scarce. All of our uncles had to go to this war. At that time the W.P.A. Road- workers put in a new road up at Laurel Run Hill and that entertained us three boys and the road workers got a big kick out of us. Dad worked at a strip mine very close to our land and that entertained us also. With 4-H, things at church, river fishing, and camping, we had a lot of fun along with the hard work.

School years

We went to school by school bus and our driver's name was Johnny Campbell. The bus would turn and go down Laurel Run Hill, down the Hollow, across Hocking River Bridge over to Route 33, and up to Red Row (named by a group of companies owned by Natco Tile and Brick). Then it would turn in front of the Shell station and go toward Nelsonville to another little brick town and row or company houses called Village of Diamond. A lot of our school buddies lived in Diamond and the row of houses across Highway 33 from the brick plant. The bus would turn back toward Haydenville, turn at a Sohio gas station at Laurel Run road, back over Hocking River, make a right turn, and go up the long winding hill called Lime Bank Hill. The bus would drop down a road toward our school called Simple Creek Road where a small creek ran beside the road. There were homes on both sides of this road that went to our school named Village of Union Furnace. It was a big grade school and a high school. A state route ran toward Logan, Ohio in front of our high school where the buses loaded and unloaded all the children.

The children came from about 10 different school routes. Back then the schools with the largest amount of children were A schools and a small number of children like ours were B schools. B schools had mostly us country children. Our school was in Hocking County and at the time our school was considered a well-to-do class B school. This is because of a lot of gas and oil wells around our school area so the school got a lot of royalty funds from these wells. Union Furnace was a small town of people who worked in larger cities like Logan, Lancaster, and Columbus. I was told by the older ones at one time there were big furnaces that melted down iron ore to make iron things. I guess a labor union moved in and took over the furnaces and that's how our school and small town got their names. I think that is why our school colors were black and gold. We played basketball and it was our number 1 sport. We had track and field in which we all took a part and there was a marching band, of I would say, 80

5

students. One day a week when we were in grade school the band would march through the small town and people were out to watch the band and all the grade school children came and went through the town. I loved it just to get out of school to march on a nice day. So as years went by, me, Tom Lee, Bob, and Jim knew people who drove a long way to rent in Columbus or Lancaster and this eventually happened to us also, which I will write about later in the story. We all had our chores to do every evening at the end of the day like feeding our livestock, gathering hen eggs, getting our oil lamps filled and wicks trimmed and coal in for the night. We had kindling cut for the next day to start the kitchen stove and our drinking water had to be brought from the well. The pump had to be drained to make sure it didn't freeze in the wintertime and we all had something to do and it went like clockwork. On some hot evenings, we sat on our new porch and watched wild rabbits who came out to lick the salt of the limestone, eat clover along the sides of the roads, and just talk and relax. Nice way to end the day and get ready for his or her next day's adventures. Dad and mother put us to bed around 10 PM every night. We slept upstairs and I never thought until later on that there was only one way in or out of that upstairs so thank God no fires. There was only one old Philco radio and it took a dry cell battery to play it and we would play it to death man. I always had to listen to Jack Armstrong, Captain Midnight, Terry and the Pirates, Tom Mix, Dick Tracy, and Lone Ranger and Silver. To me, these men could save the world, haha. Rona loved Chester Field Playhouse and country and western music and loved shows on the radio. Crazy shows like Red Skelton, Baby Snooks and Abner, Jotum Down Store, Jack Benny, and Great Gilter Sleeve. There were soap operas and Saturday night's Grand Ole Oprey and homemade popcorn and tasteless cool-aid. Our house was lit up by coal oil lamps and gave off a yellow glow. One day Uncle Dow came by and gave us an Aladdin lamp with white gas and with a new long globe and we thought we were in a different world when a pure white light was lit up and how much better to see by. Now we had an old Victrola and some old records and we played

6

it to death also. Mother sent away for some Roy Acuff records and we had Stream Line Cannon Ball and Great Speckled Bird and others. We had some old thick records way back then like Two Black Crows and My Wondering Boy Tonight. Old ones came with the VIC. It got its main spring broken and one of us had to stand by it and crank it all the time to keep it playing if we wanted music that bad. We had a kitchen, one bedroom, living room, and dining room downstairs where dad and mother slept. We four children were upstairs in two bedrooms, one for Rona and one for us three boys. We remodeled the old log house and put in a big archway door, all done by cross-cut saw and recovered old lags and chinking with new drywall and we had a nice old country home at the Crossroads. When we were small we were able to run off to play next door with the Pall children and had an apple, fruit field, and trees between our house and theirs. One summer morning Rona and I along with Bob and Jim snuck over there. We had been warned not to, many times but this morning we all chanced it and were having a real good time and lots of fun. When out of the trees came Mother and she had a long switch and was she mad. There was a black ash road that ran from Pall's house and through our farm yard. Buddy, we started to move out for home on the slick coal dust road and Rona was a little on the plump side and had a thin summer dress on and me, Bob and Jim had shorts on running right behind her. I still can see Rona doing an Indian dance and Mother was running alongside us giving us all a taste of her switch. I'll never forget every time Rona's feet hit the black dirt road, her bare feet and the black dust were flying up and I was getting my legs switched along with Bob and Jim. That stopped us from going without asking. The county road was moved across to the other side of the old washed-out road and they told Dad if you take care of it you can use it. That was right down Dad's alley. He told us boys to cut fence posts and get the old post hole digger and of all places to put a barbed wire fence was right down the middle of the old road bed. Talk about hard digging there were all kinds of bricks and road fill. We made a big front yard of it and back then Dad would send us boys down Laurel Run Hill to Grandpa Doodle's farm and go up in the hay loft and get burlap bags or sacks of hayseed a mixture of every hayseed that came out of a hay field that would fall off hay and no grass seed at all dad didn't care just as long as it came up green. We would just seed the whole front yard with the hayseed from clover to thistles. Anyways, it was green and we kept it cut. Well, we didn't have money to buy good grass seed but it looked good from a distance so we made out with a new front yard by using the old road bed. The wild rabbits and tame ones too loved to hop around and eat in the yard. I had a 4-H project on raising rabbits and in two years we had 80 or 90 mixed colors hopping around in our yard and it was a pretty sight to see them in the green grass. Chet Six was the meat manager of a big meat market in Nelsonville and he told Dad if us boys would kill and skin the rabbits he would take them all. So, we did and I think they gave us 1.50 each for them but we didn't have to cut hay or clover and buy pellets for them any longer. We had gotten tired of taking care of them and with winter coming on and no hay put up in the barn to feed them all, it was a good idea. I did love to just watch them play and hop around but got lazy and didn't want to take care of them any longer. That was the end of my 4-H project. We loved tame rabbits fried brown and put in an eight-quart pressure cooker and cooked until ready to fall from the bones and good gravy along with it. Mother and Rona could cook up good meals with homemade bread, drop biscuits, or grease biscuits. It was so good to put gravy and sausage canned in mason jars over them. Man, good. They made home-baked pies and cake also. Like I said earlier in this letter or book you could count on Sunday meals being chicken or meatloaf. You could count on one of those meat dinners along with Jello pie cake, it was very good. As I said we came to our big kitchen table and dishes were passed around from person to person after the thanks prayer. No one could leave the table until everyone had finished. Now at Christmas time, it was special to us and no school until New Year and we all helped make homemade candy of all kinds and cookies and popcorn balls, two weeks before Christmas Mother told us 3 boys to go down Laurel Run to Mr. Vance Wolfe's place and cut a tree. His place was an old tree farm and he always gave us one each year along with his son Lawrence who had a girl who also rode our school bus. We would take our sleds and saw and sometimes we had to cut a top out of a larger one to get what we wanted to use. Now with no electricity Mother had old bulbs that were beautiful, given to her by her mother, and had icicles of tin foil. We always took those things off the tree from year to year to year. There was red and green crape paper roping that hung from the four corners of the room and into the center to a large red paper bell. Each corner had a small colorful bright bulb. There was a homemade wreath hanging on the window and on the door. Like I have said before times were hard for us back then but Mother and Dad did manage to give us one large gift each and two or three small ones. We got one from our school classmates in drawing names and the gifts were no more than 35 cents. We also got one at the exchange at Church plus a sack of candy, English walnuts, and an orange or tangerine. Our Church always put on a live Christmas play of the birth of baby Jesus and always had a packed building at Christmas before that day. On Sunday night about 30 young girls and boys put on the play and were all dressed up like wise men and so on. We never will forget things like that and Mother and Mildred put us children right at our part in the play. Now on New Year's Eve, at midnight and at the change from the old year to the new one all of us families burned our Christmas trees and made New Year's wishes. Don't really know if mine ever came true or not.

Mother would give us 5 or 6 pennies for Sunday school and when we got to our Church house Mother would go right on in and we boys a little bit later when the last bell would ring. This gave Bob a little time to run over to the service station and spend 1/2 of his offering on some candy and maybe peanuts and got away with it for a long time and then got told on. We walked home almost every Sunday at noon unless someone gave us a ride to the Crossroads and when we walked home we boys would take a skinny dip swim under Laurel Run bridge, to cool off and put our Sunday clothes back on and acted like nothing ever happened.

We, Laurel Run and Wolfe boys were always together doing something like water snake hunt a lot and get in the Laurel Run creek that ran along the road and killed as many snakes out sunning themselves everywhere. Some of the snakes were large and others were small and we had green clubs and rocks to hit them and they sometimes would get hurt and come after us and we beat them to death. We saw a medium size snake in the water swimming under a flat slab of sandstone and I told Chet Wood to turn the rock over so I could see and hit the snake, I was poking muddy water with my club and don't know how I did it but I flipped that snake up and around Chet's bare neck and he did a war dance for us until the snake slid off, haha, boys will be boys at times and try anything. Also in the winter time, we would skate on a large pond of frozen ice and could see catfish swimming just under the ice at the top of the water, get a large rock and slam down on it and it would stun the catfish and we had ice axes and saws and cut through to get him and put him on our sleds and I don't know how many we took home and cleaned and froze them for later.

In the summertime, the water would start drying up and be about 2 feet deep and we all had old number 3 wash tubs and cut the bottom out of them. We used these as traps for the fish. We had old shoes on to not cut our feet on something. We could see schools of fish swimming ahead and spin and throw the tub and when it landed 2 or 3 nice fish were trapped in the wash tub and we reached down and caught them. Many of them were swimming ahead of us so we couldn't miss them. We loved to hunt for mushrooms and loved to eat them too.

Along the Hocking River was a great place to find big corn cobs and mushrooms. I remembered one year that the river, I mean Hocking River, overflowed and left scores of corn cobs and mushrooms by the thousands, and the river bottom fields were a mass of them and people came in pickup trucks and took loads of them away. I saw these at Diamond corn fields. Man, never saw that again, only that one summer in my whole lifetime. For mother, we would chop up some mushrooms into small pieces and also cut up oysters and mix with crackers along with two chicken eggs and mix and make like salmon patties and fry them in a big old iron skillet and talk about a rich sandwich. Sometimes we boys would pick wild strawberries and clean them for Mother and she would make a homemade shortcake, wasn't that a sweet treat with milk or whipped cream on top? When green tomatoes started to turn ripe we would cut and fry them in a skillet and along with green cucumbers that were also very good dipped in a flour and egg batter. We had a lot of things back then that mother and sister Rona made for a meal that was so good.

Most of us boys liked to sit on the front seat right behind the school bus driver and talk to them like Johnny Campbell, Had McVey, Bugs McDaniel, and so on. One morning it was in the fall and there was a big fog that came up from the riverbed and you could only see at the end of your nose. When we went back up to Gene and Fred Mormins, near Red Row we had to make a U-turn across Route 33 and toward the Diamond to pick up those children. Johnny Campbell has no relation to our Campbell side of the Campbells, and also his dad was one of my favorite school teachers in history and math. When Johnny was to turn he had to cross 33 and the fog was as thick as I have ever seen it, because our big bus took so long to make a U-turn he opened the door and said "Tom, get out there and listen for traffic and give me the go-ahead to cross the highway on this turnaround." I got off the bus and the motor was making a lot of noise and I listened but I could hear all kinds of noises from every place like Natco Tile Company, so I jumped back on board the bus after I gave our driver the OK to go and slid in a seat just behind him. Just as soon as we were about halfway across the highway a big tractor truck coming slow had to slam his truck to a stop a few feet from our bus. We were nearly loaded on this long 54-passenger bus and then in this heavy fog I think eight cars hit the back end of his tractor-trailer truck. We and our school had to go to court and tell our story but from that foggy morning the fog was so heavy and if we had waited for the fog to lift we would never have made it to school. No one was hurt that morning. Denny and I went out back after school was over to get a front seat on our bus. So, we squeezed behind the big garage doors and got a front seat, most of the 10 buses were down in front of the school building and we had a good idea to get on the bus in the big garage and our driver would come and get the bus and take it down front. So, we kept waiting and waiting for our driver to get our bus and we sure had the front seat. Well unknown to us our bus wasn't running well and they used another bus to take our route, Denny and I were sitting in the garage in a broken-down bus and after a long while I knew something was wrong so we got out of the bus, and out of the garage and went around in front of the school building and all the buses were loaded and gone, haha. He and I walked all the way home and Mildred called the school and reported that Denny hadn't got home from the bus and was worried so we went to see the superintendent the next day about that and that our bus driver didn't notice us not on his new bus the end of the day. So that ended the front-seat rides.

Short stories of the boy's fun

When living at the crossroads on Laurel Run Hill Dad would get a dry cell for our old Philco upright, a good short wave, and every night when we got off the school bus we boys just had to make a dash for the radio and listen for captain midnight and Tom mix. Jack Arm Strong and Dick Tracey and Terry and The Pirates. Just a few so when we heard all of these stations Rona had her turn. She enjoyed the Chesterfield Supper Club and shows like that. We had to take turns and we boys hated them but we had to let her have a turn also.

We made our own wooden cars and trucks and made wheels out of wood checkers. No plastics yet so everything was wood. Bob and Jim had new Radio Flier Wagons and a real nice place to ride down the big hill that was made smooth from coal trucks that hauled out of the strip mines. Their wagons would coast way passed Grandpa's house and man was it a long walk back uphill to the Cross Roads where we lived.

I loved to squirrel hunt and while the season lasted as I told before in this book I spent a lot of hours in the woods we had all around our home. Our yard and gardens looked nice I thought as you would drive by with a big mowed yard and dad had us three mixing up whitewash with water and lime dust and we had every tree and fence post painted. It was a cheap way to make homemade quick paint to make everything white like our barn and other buildings and also our apple trees up so far. It was clean looking against all of our green yard and when the sun was out. When we had rain in the summer time it turned to a dark gray color and when the sun came back out hot the whitewash was nice and bright again. One day I used an excuse of staying home from school to whitewash our barn so Dad and Mother let me use a wallpaper brush to whitewash it with, we lived about 7 miles from our school grounds so I could hear a thunderstorm over toward our school and could see the dark clouds over that way but I used the excuse I painted our barn white with homemade whitewash and my teacher said how could you whitewash in all the rain we had here yesterday Tommy Lee. I stuck to my excuse and said it didn't rain at our place all day teacher. Ha

Three boys knew, like an eight-day clock, we could expect the Lewis Thompson and Todd's girls and others would come to check on the mail for their mothers. Plus, some of them rode our school bus and just had to come after mail to check on what was going on at the three Huddy Boy's place. I remember my old farmer school teacher sometimes would say to our class, "I got 4 sons going out or over to die for this great nation and not allowed to vote for it until the age of 21." I'll never forget that I loved him as a teacher. His name was Perry Campbell but not related to our Campbell family. He had a big farm out on Zion Ridge near us and the fire tower. He'd come into our classroom a big lanky farmer teacher and a good one and have these homemade teachers paddles with holes drilled in them and say to us in the class of 45 children. "If I can't beat it in your heads, I'll beat it in your bottoms." He could do it too. We all respected P.C. Campbell.

On top of Laurel Run Hill, I thought it was the hottest, driest place to live and we set our house down at the crossroads, and with all the woods around us, not much air flowed. When a car came by our place along would come road dust and come right inside our house. Rona and Mother had to always dust and wax our furniture with Johnson's wax because our windows were open and everything seemed to be sucked indoors. Because of that dust problem we boys just had to go to the creek, down near Emmit Forest's farm, which was mostly spring water and swamp but always flowing and cold. We dug a large size hole where a big pipe carried water to the other side of the road. It was about 1/2 mile from our place and we had it damned up to about 3-4 ft. deep and man was it cold. On a hot summer day when it was around 90 degrees out it was nice swimming but, on the walk, up the road to home we almost melted. Sometimes we would put a number 3 washtub out in the yard and see who could duck and hold our breath the longest. To think just 2 and 1/2 miles to good old cool Hocking River just flowing by but we were too young to go there without older ones to watch after us. When we did get older and larger look out Old Man Hocking River. We really used up the old Hocking River in our young lives. Down below the big hill was a small creek that ran off the Todd's farm and Wiggin's place and we had to go to Grandpa's place to get all the water to make a cold creek swimming pool. That creek was the Laurel Run Creek that ran always along Laurel Run Road to Hocking River along with Lime Bank Hill Creek. It went by the Norris and VanBibber place, where we did all the brown water snake hunting it was full of them and we made a lot of kills there. Just something to do.

Everyone who lived on Laurel Run Road had dogs, some that wanted to eat you up so we were always ready for them when we passed their driveway or lane. There was always a big dog and a small one to keep his nerve up to come charging after us so we were ready with some rocks and clubs for the attack. This one hot afternoon I was walking over to Route #33 to catch the Lake Shore bus and go to Nelsonville and back. It was Raining off and on so Mother had me use a big old umbrella like today's beach ones. I was walking right along and it stopped raining so I took the umbrella down and I just remembered the two biters John Norris had so I thought to myself I'll use this for a club. I had another idea that when they were almost on me I would let that big umbrella pop open. I was on the far side of the road and here they came charging across the road at me. I popped the umbrella open and you wouldn't in all this world see two dogs stop so fast and run backward like a cougar was after them and run backward crying and barking. That broke the habit of coming after us and they couldn't figure out that big balloon popping open when they were almost to me. I wish I would've had that on a camera reel. By the way the bus ride to Nelsonville was around 35 cents, even on umbrella day. Everyone had dogs and one day a mad dog came down our Laurel Run road and did a number on all the dogs and we had to kill them. I had my old squirrel single-shot gun I hated to do it but they asked me to shoot them and I did. We had to bury them all afterward and that thinned out all the dogs from our place at the top of the hill to Hocking River Bridge. Man, a lot of good dogs and some mean ones had to be killed. No one was out and all of us children were in school when the mad dog came by. Every once in a while, a mad fox would come in the yards foaming at the mouth and wasn't afraid of man or dog and was staggering and glassy-eyed too. We had to shoot old Rex, our Grandpa's big white dog and boss of Laurel Run in his hay day. I remember the Ryan family all had to take shots around their belly button because a mad dog bit their dog, they all had to be taking the painful shots just in case one of them was scratched by their house dog who was bitten. We three boys had to be careful about all the wild animals we had locked up in pens and cages. We put them right in cages and didn't know if they may have been bitten before we caught them and penned them up. Well, we didn't think of things like that. God took care and looked after us.

We had a lot of flower beds around our house and Mother was always getting flowers, shrubs, and trees from places. She would send away to seed companies and get some that way too. She loved sunflowers, four O clocks, pansies, and roses of all colors. Big snowball bushes, little button white bushes, pussy willow trees, a lot of fruit trees, and concord grape arbors were all so good come fall. Plus, we made apple cider and homemade jelly, and the works when we could get the sugar to can with. We also had gooseberry and currant berry. She made jelly from wild crab apples and other wild fruits. So, having them was very good in the wintertime. We also picked many apples, Pa pas, and elderberries for jelly. Pa pas were shaped like a stubby banana and too sickeningly sweet. My favorite berry was black raspberry that grew wild and a lot of them if you could beat the wild birds to them. Mother and Rona liked strawberries best. We also had rhubarb and I loved to get me a big stock and a handful of coarse salt and man a good treat to us all. Plus, a pie now and then. Mother was great at baking homemade bread and biscuits and we always had that with homemade jelly of some sort to piece on at near bedtime.

16

We three slept in a room at the crossroads and in the wintertime, it was downright cold at night. The only registers were the ones dad cut in the floor of our rooms and the heat coming up the stairway but we slept in a big feather tic mattress bed and stayed cozy. When Bob would be taken to Aunt Pauline and Uncle Dow's to visit for a week they would take him to Nelsonville movies and he would tell us about the whole movie. When Mother put coal in the stove she could hear us boys, through the grates, talking and say alright it's time to get to sleep and save that story until tomorrow. We loved to share our stories with each other and really get into the movie story like we were in it. Then off into dreamland we would go. Now if we had a great day coming up like going to a family reunion or a county fair it was hard to shut it down and go to sleep. We would wish our night was already over so we could get to it. I really don't know how other buddies and pals who had no one to grow up with and play and fuss with lived. I always wondered about that, it seems lonely to me.

We all had our own area to build bridges, roads, houses, and barns and you had to ask your brother to use his road to cross his bridges and properties to get to our area. Sometimes we had to pay a toll to cross his bridge so we had a handful of limestone from the new road that we used for money to pay the tolls. At times we would get fighting and I remember Bob's homemade truck caved Jim's homemade bridge in and made Jim mad so he took a hammer and smashed one of Bob's bridges in and the fight was on. The last thing I saw was Jim chasing Bob down the road with Dad's hatchet and trying to hit him. He couldn't catch him so they ran I don't know how far until it turned funny and a while later here they came and good buddies again. We brothers loved each other but had our misunderstandings at times and the fight was on. I loved my two-playing brothers even when they made me pay tolls for crossing their land and using their bridges and roads. A pocket of small lime stones off the road wasn't too bad to pay but man don't you happen to move or break down a bridge or it would come the end of the world and the fight was on. They would take a hammer to the other roads, to get even, that we had made for hours and smash it to kingdom come just playing. We had tons of room on the old yellow clay bank to call our own and you could set your own rules and charges. Mother would dress us in short pants, no shoes, and barebacked and we would play for hours and be burned to almost black by the sun. We had big shade trees shading us from the real hot summer sun and in the evening Mother would call us into bathtubs and get to bed to get recharged for the next day's toll charge games. Who knew what we may dream up in our minds at dream time?

We were the busiest 3 boys you ever saw and always looking for something to do like high walking stilts we made and we would have to climb on them off the porch railing. They were long and high up and we would come down the W.P.A made slope. It was long and steep and we were on ten-foot-high stilts. We would have to lean back and start down over the slope and look out ahead of you and man you sure were up there. It seemed like only sky and if you would fall or jump you'd be up to a 10- or 15-foot fall and it was a long way down but we loved it. God looked after us well.

I may have told this before but we boys always had something going on. When we would feed our mother chickens and shell corn for them we would stick a chicken's neck and head under its wing and hold it for a few seconds and they would go right to sleep. It doesn't hurt them any. Then we had a lot of young fryers to raise from small biddies mother sent away for and they would come by mail and just peep when delivered to mother. We 3 boys had a lot of young chickens so when they came near us after corn we would pick them up and put their heads under their wing and they would go to sleep and we would just see how many we had just laying around sleeping. The rest of the flock was still eating so we took our foot, flipped them over so they would come too and go back to eating with the others. We called them young fryers when butchered at a certain size. Then we would cold pack them and when you were ready for a Sunday chicken dinner you would get 2 or 3 mason jars to open and dump out the broth and chicken all nice and tender ready to roll in flour and fry.

Back in those days with no electricity to cook and save meat, mason jars were the only way to go except for sugar cured hams and smoked them also. Mother would fix our breakfast some mornings and send one of us down in the cellar to get a 2-gallon jar of sausage balls and pour them in a hot skillet over a coal range and we would have homemade biscuits or drop biscuits and some gravy on a cold winters morning and man that's good eating. See it took a lot of work for everyone to get all the jars washed and scalded, but was well worth it when it was opened on a winter cold day. Nice to have good cooks. Now I remember when the 8-quart steam canner came around and when we went from our old lard cans to a pressure cooker it was like night and day. We would put 8 quarts in it at a time and set them out to cool off and you could hear the lids popping and scaling and done. Mother and Aunt Pauline both got one each and we also cooked many meat meals in them.

When Halloween time rolled around we all from the top of Laurel Run Hill to Red Row and down through Wolfe Basin and up Campbell's lane hit every house and soaped windows and also did things we shouldn't have done. We got carried away like unhooking goats out of pens, opened up kitchen doors, and ran them inside. We turned off outside electric switch boxes and people would go out to find the electric box. Some place in the house they would find their goats in a dark room along with a lot of squealing going on and we were long into the next target. Back then no one took their switch keys out of the switch to their cars and one night the older ones like young married ones had a big party. We hit them way after dark and pushed about 20 cars from along the main road. We pushed one at a time way down the road bumper to bumper while the party was going on. Then we hit them with corn and fodder shocks on the porch and turned off the lights and we younger boys ran and when the older men came out to run us down no one had a car to chase us with. It

19

was funny then but the police were brought in on this one and when all was said and done they found out who all of us were and dropped the charges. I do hate the one that we went too far with Madam Melle a real Gypsy who had a big ball of glass on a table in a small place of business or shop. The front door was unlocked and we could all see her sitting in her chair looking into the big glass ball. We had a large group of us that night when we were making our rounds from house to house. I think it was brother Bob who opened the door and pitched a handful of shelled field corn in on her and she had a 38-caliber revolver and came out mad. We ran in every direction in the dark while she was cussing and emptying her handgun in all directions with bullets bouncing off the brick highway to Route 33. We were very lucky not one of us was hit. It was not good to do that to her at all.

At our big Campbell reunions every summer a large, large group of the Campbells, Vollumers, Huddys, Taylors, Wends, and Mounts had a lot of great things to eat and we children had our wading clothes on. Out in front of Grandma and Grandpa's house, there was a 2-foot-deep small pond or hole in which cold water ran year-round. Uncle Charley put a 22-pound blue catfish into it that he caught on a trotline on the river fishing a week before our reunion. That was more fun to try to grab the slick catfish, let alone handle a 22-pounder. All of us children were soaking wet, the dozen or more of us. We all seemed to get a hold of him but he was too big and heavy to lift up and out, such fun for all ages.

When I was young I had my turn to go spend a night with our cousins and had fun because they were a little older than we were and had a lot of things to play with, like, bikes and roller skates with a rink upstairs in the garage or big barn. They had a pony named Mousy and we went over to Pattonville and fished for big catfish and picked wild strawberries. Aunt Vesper and Gerald were so kind and good to us and went to the Church of God with all of us at Laurel Run and it saddens me to say I helped dig her grave at Wolfe's family cemetery in 1948. I remember it well and that she suffered greatly bless her heart. A small aunt in size but a great one to us all. So, God took her on home and Don, Ray, and Uncle Gerald were left behind with us. I've seen most all of the Campbell boys go on and have wives and children with some still here. I loved each one of them. A large family to know them all and all loved to see and talk about what had taken place since the last reunion.

We boys loved it when thrashing of wheat came to our farms and big steel wheeled steam engines pulled a big metal thrasher and set up to thrash our wheat and put that big long straw pipe up high to blow the straw in a big pile so we could climb up it and play, fun. Then Dad and his brother Dow and workers from the state institutions would all work hard on thrashing and bailing straws. You would have to see all those bags of wheat at the end of the day. They would take the thrashcr pipcs down and what a big pile of blown straw was ready to be all bailed up and put on wagons and tractors. They would take a bailed straw to one of the big red barns used for cow and horse bedding during the winter months. The big belts were taken off the steam engine tractors, hooked back on the thrasher, and were done for another year. OK, away it went to some other farm, and the man that owned the outfit tractor and thrasher was related to us, his name was Ed Gagg, and had married into the Huddy family.

Grandpa Huddy had a big team of horses. One was black and one was red and we loved to get on the big hay wagon they pulled and go 10-15 miles out in the country. That's called country fun. Of course, when we had our hay rides we would have the wiener roasts and marshmallow parties. I loved the rides and eating and playing at the halfway point. Then put out our fire, load up, and head home with the lanterns hanging from the wagon for tail lights. We would have worn ourselves out and were ready for bed. Those were good times and we had all kinds of games back then like kick the can, drop the handkerchief, red rover, and hide and seek. Fun games and ball games along with the big long wagon with hay, people, and children, hanging and sitting everywhere. You don't see too much of that nowadays, do you? No.

The Athens County Fair

A big, big fun day for us boys. Mother and Dad parked the big 2-ton truck across the fairground on the other side of the race track and in the shade but it made it a long walk to where all the action was. We all knew when it was lunch or dinner time to meet at the truck to eat. We couldn't afford the cost of hamburgers and fish sandwiches because we were poor along with others. Rona and Mother cooked up a good meal I remember it like it was yesterday. We had cooked tame rabbit and gravy cooked in a big pressure cooker and potato salad and baked beans. Man good. That saved us more money to spend so we three boys and Rona got 2.00 each and right to the penny arcade we would go where everything was a penny. Such fun. We found a big shade tree near our truck with picnic benches and there was always a nice table for us. Very few people like horse jockeys came by so we all would wear ourselves out by firecracker night and come on home and show each other our penny arcade cards and trinkets. It was a great day each fall and the races were free so we could just watch them from the bleachers that were built on a hill, but the sun would burn you up. I love the horse-pulling teams with all their pretty harnesses on and ivory white, fancy-looking team from the pony team to the big work and logging farm team weighing well over a ton a piece and could they pull. I loved horses so much.

At the Athens county fair, I got my first look at the two trucker cars and watched them go around the fair tracks and they were so far ahead of anything I ever saw. They looked like they came out of Buck Rogers or Flash Gordon funny papers. They had this one big headlight in the grill and whichever way you turned the steering wheel this light would rotate with the steering wheel. It had a long sleek body, wire spoke chrome wheels and wow it was something else. It would cruise along at 130 miles per hour and wow what a car. The only ones I have ever seen were burgundy red and one was sky blue. It was a dream car to us boys and we spent a lot of the time talking to the salesmen asking questions. I've seen two and have seen them run and you may never see one but only a picture of it. I'm sorry that it never hit the nation like it did Bob, Jim, and I.

Uncle Wiley and the Ryan family farm

I want our readers to know my Uncle Wiley, Ryan, and Aunt Ivalou, my Dad's sister. They lived on the big farm near Chauncey and near Hocking and the plains. Uncle Wiley helped work on his dad's and his Uncle Charley's farm. He had a small house that he built for Ivalou that nearly choked us all to death. Only God was behind that, they were in their late 80s. You can read the rest of the story in my book story. My class school friend Harold Todd happened to stay home from school the same day I did and he and his dad and mother lived across from his old gram ma and gram pa and saw the smoke coming up from their old home and no one was home at his place and he tried to get them to come out and they ran upstairs and wouldn't come down and Harold had no phones yet in that area so he runs to our place crying and shouting for help. When they were first married, had hardships like the rest of us back then. Uncle Wiley got a job on the railroad in a small town called Corning. The job was on the railroad yard switching train cars from track to track and one day the engineer never read the hand sign and Uncle Wiley was in between two cars. He was hooking up the air and took a quick push, Uncle Wiley dove from out between the coal cars and made it all but one leg that was crushed off just below the knee joint. When all was said and done Uncle Wiley got I think around $24,000.00 for what had happened and back then it was a pile of money. He had his dad and his dad's brother sell the big Ryan farm to him and his wife Ivalou. The old Ryan brothers and mother all moved to Athens and out of the big farmhouse and man a big one it was. Wiley and Ivalou remodeled it from basement to roof. They put in new hardwood floors and the works it became a real lovely home. Uncle and Aunt now owned everything. There were livestock, pigs, milk cows, chickens, and even dogs. The older Ryans moved to Athens with only a few personal things on their backs. Uncle Wiley hobbled around on one leg and had to go to Cincinnati Ohio to try on a new leg made from plastic I think. We and our cousins lived in the small house on the hill that was my Aunt and Uncle's first home that he built after they married. Mother stayed with all of us until they got back after the fitting of the leg. Three railroad lines came down around the farm and a lot of tramps and hobos came around. They saw the big barns and sheds as a good place to sleep and catch another freight train the next day. Lord only knew what all of them took from the remodeled home out toward the tracks. The railroad was New York Central, Pennsylvania, and Hocking Valley, and there were miles of coal cars and box cars passing day and night. One hot summer evening we had the doors open and only the screen door for cool air, the Ryans had a mean Chow dog and a big crossbred dog and they were lying on the porch sleeping, and all of a sudden we heard a man cussing the dogs and said he was bitten on the leg and wanted to know where he was and the largest city around and the two big watchdogs got him and he was still cussing as he went back over the hill toward the railroad tracks. Uncle Wiley hired Dad to help work on the big farmhouse and a lot of the time I would go along with him and help out. Aunt Ivalou really put the money on that big home and man was it turning out real nice. The oldest girl Shirley, a favorite of mine had already gotten married and lived up in the city of Columbus where she and her husband had good jobs. Lenny was still at home but had a good job with Southeastern Electric Company back then. A son named Jack Ryan, who was the same age as me, helped also with the new home for his mother. Then along came the youngest, Tom Ryan who helped. The house was just beautiful and also the Ryan family moved off the hill and out of that small house that started it all. We three boys took turns going to Ryan's farm to visit maybe two days at a time and were warned at home to not do a lot of things as the Ryan boys did. ha… They were not mean to us or anything but got into things. They had a big rooster who was a cock of the farm and he would chase you and flog you if he had the chance to around his lady chickens. One day Len said we'll take the pride out of him and we ran him down and painted his wing a John Deer green and tail feathers also. He ran under the new chicken building and it burned down and the rooster, his wings back there were no feathers at all. They burned off but still looked like a cock rooster with his feathers all up front and he still owned the farm. It didn't bother him to look like a Christmas-baked chicken, haha. The boys would ride milk cows and have milk fights in the barn while milking and squirt the barn cats right in the face from the utter. Sometimes young cows would get excited and jump over the bottom door to get away. Little Tommy climbed up on the barn and took off the weather in vain. I was there once and had to yell "Your tractor is coasting over the hill!" to Len who had forgotten to set the brake. Off it went, a brand-new farm tractor, Len tried to stop it but it turned over and smashed the hood, exhaust pipes, and grill. We were all thankful Len couldn't get on it or catch it before it turned over because he may have gotten hurt. Uncle and Aunt were down in Athens shopping while we played at the farm. That was one more thing that happened on the farm. Ivalou and Wiley really treated us well back then and had money to spend on treats at the drive-in, restaurant, and sandwich shops. I got my first taste of a foot-long Coney and man I loved it in the city of Athens. One day when they took us swimming in the Athens pool they stopped afterward for a snack. Later on, after a few years when Dad was down with his stomach and couldn't work so that is when Ivalou and Wiley took us into the little house on the hill, Bob and Jim were put in the Chauncey Dover School that year. I don't know yet if Brother Jim liked it or not. Bob was doing ok and had a girlfriend named June Hammond. It was a rough time and tough winter on us and Uncle let us use a milk cow and had chicken eggs and meat out of the meat house so what great help from the Ryans back in the 1947-1948 time. Bob stayed with the Ryan family to finish out his school year. That's when I pulled two wagon loads to Wiggins' place on that cold winter day. One day Uncle Wiley told Tom and me "I wish I had my leg back. I would give all the money back for my leg". He was good to me and I to him. I would take him or drive him to work at times and he would tell me what he would like to have done while he was away. He had a lot of trust in me. I would go to Athens

27

to pick up a hog and steer and butcher the hog and beef cattle and skin them and hang them up and get them ready to cut up and also render lard and I love to chew on what we called cracklins that last for a long time. All day if you wish. Aunt Ivalou would fry up the tenderloins from along hogs backbone have homemade bread and always had enough to feed an army. She also cooked fresh liver and onions, and good, man. We would never go hungry around the Ryan table and what good food. We Huddy boys and Ryan boys helped scrape off the hog's hair to get it ready to be cut up and that was a big job. We loved it.

The plane crash story

Here's a story that comes back to me. One afternoon a summer rain storm came up and we boys were hoeing one of our gardens, an airplane came by overhead and the motor was sputtering badly and we boys said to one another "must be something wrong with its motor." It was flying low and a storm was coming up so we stopped hoeing and we went inside on that Saturday evening. That night I stayed all night with my pal Chester Wood and in the early morning, his dad Chuck said that an airplane crashed over next to the hill near Sand Run. We all went right over to see where it had crashed and had to manage some of the hills to get there. I was a young boy at that time so this plane was the one that we saw last evening fly over our place with motor trouble during the rain storm. It was a 5-passenger plane and tried I guess to find a field or opening to land but no luck, and it came down through the tree tops and clipped their tops off and came to a creek bottom. It just tore the five men on board to small pieces and there were parts of their bodies lying every place and parts of the plane also. I picked up a few small pieces of the airplane. The law enforcement got to the crash and cleared everyone out of the area. What a mess with the motor of the plane lying in the water of the small country creek and it took the lives of the five businessmen going somewhere. I saved my parts from the plane for years.

The locks and the Church of God

When my mother was a young girl she lived in the old home place that grandpa and grandma built when they were first married. It had a creek flowing along it from up in the Wolfe Hollows where two creeks ran together. Grandpa Herbert had a barn put up on the side of the hill with a small road going on up to Bert Hill's old place and Bud Wolfe's place also. The old canal that came down through Newark and on down to Haydenville and Nelsonville had locks to raise water deep enough to float barges and was pulled by horses and mules on what was called towpaths. When they came to a barge coming in the other direction they had to unhook horses, mules, and oxen pass by each other and hook them all back up again. The locks were right behind the Sohio station and then the Hocking Valley Railroad and our Church of God were all right near each other. Our Church was called South Haydenville Locks Church of God. Back then our grandpa Campbell went and fired up the furnace downstairs outside the stairway to have it nice and warm for everyone by the time we started Sunday school and afterward Church. Our attendance ran I would say from 75 to 80 people gathering to worship our God. On a hot summer evening cars would pass by on the gravel road out front of the building and we of course would have the windows open or up and the screen windows in for air, was it ever hot? Cars would pass by and a cloud of dust would come in and out the other side and we all had hand funeral fans to try to stay cool. Thank God Grandma Campbell, Mother and Aunts Mildred and Aunt Vesper Vollumer along with some other older saints helped us young ones to learn about our great God. It didn't bother us three Huddy boys to walk home. We had a large young people group also around 25-30 and all went to our school or to Logan. We had good times with always something going on like wiener roasts, marshmallows, and ball games.

Living, work, war, and war efforts

It seemed to me we were out of touch with the outside world and the 2nd World War was going on and saw all those bombers like B-17 and B-29 in formation flying over our place somewhere. All of our young uncles had gone off to war to fight and the only way we heard of it was the old radio and Sunday paper and the letters they wrote home.

We had no electricity or inside running water at all. We had to go out to get the water and coal and to the cellar for canned foods or out in our gardens. In other homes about a mile away they had bathrooms and inside running water and just flick a switch on the wall and you had lights. We had three coal-oil lamps to trim wicks and fill every night, clean up the old smoky globes, and use the old yellow lamps for our studies and homework. Same old simple way of like each day we all had our chores to do but to me, we had to battle for things we had the hard way that cut us off from the rest of the world. Not only us but others way out in the boondocks and the only news on the radio was Loule Thomas or Paul Harvey or some other newsman on our box. I'm still here today telling my stories thanks to God that seen us through.

When one of our uncles or family was home on leave and told of his experiences in the Army, Navy, or Marines we wanted to hear their stories. I loved all my uncles, like Uncle Paul, Uncle Pete, Foster, and Dad's brother Jim Huddy. They all had stories to tell to us and I was all ears. I'm just sitting here thinking of things that slipped my mind way back when we were growing up at home. Dad got new cut green lumber from Nub Loomis over on Simple Creek where he had a sawmill set up and could saw up newly cut oak trees. If you built a new hog house do it that day while you could drive spikes and nails and just let them dry up and you have to drill the boards with a hand drill then to get the nail through it. The sun would warp the green lumber so bad, so Dad had us boys sorting out straight boards to build with. All are cut with an old cross-cut or rip hand saw. Once you got the hog pen nailed together it would take a bulldozer to tear it apart. Plus, Dad wanted it whitewashed, haha. Everything green turned white and I always loved our changing four seasons and we did go out and gather wild berries and nuts, put them in barrels, and use them. Black walnuts for Christmas candies at that time and we just plain made our foods from scratch. We had to make food from scratch during the five years of World War II and we were rationed on a lot of things like sugar and coffee, rubber from tires and gas and you couldn't buy a leather or rubber basketball for love or money man. Dad and mother got us by. We younger ones stayed here at home to help out by helping out at school with iron scrap drives. We gathered up any steel or iron farmers had sitting rusted down and hauled it to school to be picked up and hauled to steel mills. There it all was to be melted down to make tanks, guns, ships, and warfighting tools for our fighting armies. I was in charge of our bus route and man the iron we hauled on big old trucks to our school you wouldn't believe it and we had 8 bus routes besides our little town. Everyone pitched in and there were other things we did to help like bring in milkweed pods that they made life jackets out of. During the school breaks all of us boys helped in any way, we could. Like a great Japanese officer said, "We've awakened a sleeping giant". Then a lot of things we were used to having were taken away from us and shipped to our fighting men overseas to help out in the war. We couldn't buy tires for car rims or any other kind of rubber. We could only get so much sugar per child per month. People could get very little gas if any and everything was cut back a lot. You had to get a permit to buy a new bike. If you could find one you had to show you needed it to ride to work and let them know how many miles you had to peddle back and forth to your workplace. We three brothers wanted to fix up a bike with parts we came across. We walked for miles to get to small towns around our area. We'd hear so and so had a set of handlebars and so and so had a front wheel. We got our wheel bearings at Carpenters Hardware. There were no good inner tubes and we had to use broken corn cobs and newspapers to stuff around the wheel to take the place of the tube. Friction tape was used to wrap the tire to the wheel but there was always rubbing in some places. It didn't work too well but we never gave up on a good bike until a drinking friend of Dad, saw the good tire Bob paid Rona $8.00 for and he traded Bob for it. Bob was so stingy with it and maybe he had a good reason for that. One day Bob and Jim were out at the Todd boy's place and somehow, I got two dollars together and I walked out to see if Bob would lend me his bike and then I would ride over to Route 33 and get us all some candy. He agreed to that and reminded me to make sure I took good care of the bike. He knew I was hard on things and would hardly let me ride his bike. That day I had on a big baggy pair of pants and I didn't go 50 feet until I got the pant leg hung up in the chain and fell over, so here he came for me a full blast and hitting me for upsetting his bike and I was trying to fight him off but his bike chain was still fastened to me. That was the end of the candy trip. Boy, the silly things we boys would fight about.

Dad and mother went to Columbus to work and rented a place along with Uncle Dow, Aunt Pauline, and Uncle Charley Campbell, Aunt Mildred's husband. Aunt Mildred moved and her children moved into our home at the crossroads and everyone else had jobs up in the big city of Columbus and came home on the weekends. My Aunt Mildred took good care of us Huddy's and had three of her own. We got along pretty well together with Mildred in charge of us all. I always loved her so much because she was good to all of us children and fed and took care of us all while Mother and Dad worked to make it during the 2nd World War. Uncle Dow and Aunt Pauline owned a 40-acre farm just out from our place and they worked in Columbus at an airplane factory but this didn't work out so well for us all. Mother cooked at Timken Roller Bearings and Dad worked on loading docks, then would come back home to us kids on the weekend. The 2nd World War was raging overseas and most all of my uncles were drafted and some captured and put in prison camps. They were freed, like 2 years later at the end of the war. I loved to hear their stories and still yet today remember them. I was only 10 years old that Sunday morning December 7th, 1941 and I was worried about them putting me in the army.

Start of fishing camp and river adventures

We grew up year by year and every so often Dad and Mother took us boys and Rona over to the Hocking River on a week's fishing and camping outing. We traveled in an old covered wagon with a mule pulling it. We camped on the Old Fred Stire's farm along the river. What a good time in our lives we were soon at the age that we could go river camping on our own with our school buddies and started our adventures on the river. There was a tree near the large rock by the railroad track where we had two paths come down from the railroad track to our beach camping area. We could park our trucks and cars up at the Church of God parking lot and walk down the railroad tracks, up above long corn fields that belonged to the Webb's or VanBibber's and Stire's. Now we three boys knew the river bank to bank and the bottom and riffles and how deep the water was at what spot. From the river bridge to our curve area, the river was backed up by a big rock and stone riffle that ran all the way across to a sand and gravel bar and green river willow clumps we called sand bar. Anyways the river was deep along in front of our camping area and we boys put a diving board and it reached out over the water that was 8-9 feet deep in that area. Our river row boat was locked and chained to a big white sycamore tree by the big flat rock we could fish off of a real good rock for bass fishing. Now our boat was a real nice one made by Chet Wood's dad and his uncle Bill Wood and man could they build river boats easy to row with only one nice paddle about 12 feet long and John boat style. A small creek flowed out from behind the Sid Kappel's store and we were camped about 3/4 mile up river but we could row right up to Sid's from Hocking River. We have plenty of canned foods like pork-n-beans and canned meats like Spam and a lot of other foods. Now our pop or soda drinks are put in dip nets and let down over the back of our riverboat into the water to keep them cool. It was real nice of Mother and Dad to let us charge all the camping food we used on the river to their account. I never did know until this day how much we put on that charge account but we had plenty to eat along with our fish and frogs and we sure had it made didn't we? We would stay on the river for a long time putting our days in with our daily jobs, like gathering firewood. We would push old dead willows over and break them into pieces and use them at night for campfire heat, light, and cooking. The Indians named the river, Hocking River years ago. The cooled pop went well with chips and canned Spam roasted over an open fire with a three-forked stick. We would heat pork-n-beans cooked up in a big old heavy iron skillet with Spam cut up in it and that was a real treat. In the beginning, each of us had a tree stand or platform about 4-5 feet off the ground and it was tied and nailed to four trees and we had to make ladders to climb up on it. They had log floors and we used old blankets mother gave us to kinda soften it up to sleep on. See we were off the sandy ground and away from snakes, night predators, foxes, and dogs, that way. I had a 16 gauge shotgun just in case any hobos or tramps came from the tracks snooping around maybe hungry or for anything else. We had coal oil lanterns hanging up in a tree or two someplace between our 3 platforms near to each other. You see the river would draw a lot of wild game coming in for food and drinking water and would smell where we had been cooking and come by for a closer look. We would put big logs and old stumps on the fire to make it last until dawn while we got some shut-eye and got charged up for the coming day. Large cans of fresh drinking water were kept full to cook, do our dishes, and use for washing our faces early in the morning. I want to tell you of the early morning dawns coming through the treetops, with the mist and fog coming off the river water and birds welcoming a new day. It's one of the most beautiful sights and sounds I've ever seen and heard in my life, believe me. You can enjoy these things in life when out camping like us Huddy boys did. See I can write this book and get right into my thoughts and it's just like I am there reenacting these things all over again. Thank God for letting me still remember all of these stored things in my mind to be able to tell you, the reader, of years gone by what we did on the Hocking River. It was like another world.! Now my own children can read this maybe someday about what their dad, Bob, and Jim did on the river and pass it on to their own children. Now, I am an old man going on 78 years and like Paul Harvey, I would like to tell you the Rest of the story, haha, okay, around 2 and 3 a.m. the big freight train would come by and wake us up from all the shaking of the earth. We were right near the track and the train was above us and he had to toot or blow his big fog horn before crossing at Laurel Run just ahead. Sometimes the engineer or fireman would see our bank fishing fire from way down the rail and give us boys a toot or two, haha. We were still awake when he'd come by and then it was sleep time and we would call it a day. Our new day would begin with eating a hot cooked meal and then we would check our rods and reels and bait them again. We would tie them down in case a large fish would bite and take off up or down the river and take our rods and reels along with them. Then we'd check the three trout lines that we each had with our name tag on both ends of the line tied from the bank or willow branch. At night we would jump in the river boat and go and find them that got hooked on one of our 150 hooks hanging down from a big twine line we had across the river and usually had it tied to a large willow branch about to break. We kept our bait fresh in tubs with holes in them to let the water come through it until we would re-bait our big lines. If some of the big minnow chubs happened to die we would use them anyway because old catfish didn't care if they were dead or alive and loved large minnows and chubs, haha. We also had night crawlers and soft craws and dough balls all doctored up small and each leader hanging down off large trot line string had swivels so the catfish would not twist up our big lines. We had to use weights to hold the sag down and keep the baits off the bottom. We set up three different lines with 50 hooks each for the night fishing. We used dough balls that were made with flour and water mixed and maybe a little vanilla or boiled potato and large chub minnows and crayfish we would catch with a net in the river and we had plenty of night crawlers and red worms. All we had to do was dig in the old brush and fodder brush piles that were left from earlier high water and were full of worms and had everything we needed. We did have to go get our 5-gallon cans of drinking and cooking water often and set it in the shade some to keep the hot sun off. We had good trout line bait, sometimes we would use old beef and chicken parts but we would set turtle hooks and use old spoiled meat. We loved to fish by the firelight and oil lanterns in the dark. We roasted hot dogs on a long willow stick, told jokes and stories, and listened to big river bullfrogs bellow up and down the river banks. The toads sang along with them and so did the night Katydids chirping. A fox would bark from across the river and like I mentioned before all of them came to the river to see what they could drink and eat. The critters fed on pray and like the raccoons loved crayfish and minnows and our fish also on stringers. We sometimes heard strange noises but never got too spooked with a lot of buddies with us, haha. What a good time we all had and now I'm old and so is bro Bob right behind me and most of our gang has passed on. Chet Woods, Ralph Sparks, Red Baumgardner, bro Jim and Denny, and more but we had our day in the sun and along Hocking River, and may I add to that I'd love to do it all over again just wind my life back to 15,16,17,18 years and start again. Bob, Jim, and I started real young and would go to the river without permission and swim an old muddy river off their banks, enter it, swim out in the current, and swim with trash and other things. The current quarter of a mile. We just wanted to swim in would take us way down river along the corn field maybe the swift water then we would p wade back in the same corn field to the road and get on the river bridge flooring which was still above water. There we would sink glass bottles that floated by under the bridge from maybe Lancaster or Logan or some side creek who knows. The three of us were rock throwers man and we've killed wild game by peppering anything with our sling-shot arms as fast as from one hand to the right arm and could keep the air full of rocks like a machine or

Gatling gun. We sure could heave those rocks, nice-sized rocks, and throw them out of sight up in the air.

Fishing cabin at the camp

We needed a cabin to stay in while it rained and a dry place to sleep at night and not sleep on the ground with all the crawling things of the night. We were wrong but at the time the only good place to build was on the sand bar. This one day at our curve camp site it started to rain and we had a canvas over our heads and our platforms and everything got wet. We looked across the river to the sand and gravel bar and decided to build a cabin to sleep in and get out of the rain and the job was on, haha. Now our dad had a lot of old windows and doors and tin roofing he let us have and hand tools like hammers nails, and hand saws. He had some 2 x 4s and we cut our post and used a post hole digger to put our hole deep in the sand bar and put our framework up. I think we made a 12ft by 12ft cabin and I drove our supplies in our car that had been made into a truck. We asked Carl Poling if we could use the tractor road at the end of his cornfield to get to our cabin site on the sand bar. Carl said "OK" probably because we helped him on the big Wolf and Poling farm. He paid us well and had children that were younger than we were and they rode our school bus to go to Union Furnace also. Now Carl told us Huddy boys we could have all the slabs of wood along the road and river. He had a small sawmill by the road so we all put the wood slabs in the river and it looked like an old logging camp out west. There was nothing in our way but gravel and sand and plenty of old wood back along the way for our firewood. Off to work we went and our dad talked into letting us have all of his windows, old doors, enough tin for a roof, and his hand tools. We floated slabs and swam along with them and kept them moving until they reached our sand bar and all of our gang would drag the slabs up on the sand bar to dry out under the hot sun. It was our siding for the cabin, floor, our 12 bunk beds, benches, tables, chairs, and steps up to the floor. The beds were not too bad if you put a few blankets under you. All of this we put up high above the sand bar and high-water rise would run under it. So, we put large poles deep and steel cables for guy cables to help anchor the cabin to hold steady against the flood water in case it ever got high or tried to wash it away. The waters did wash it away later on and it saddened us as we watched it go downriver in the late fall when the river came over our sand bar and a lot of hard work and fun and good times were washed away. But while it lasted what great fun we all had camping in the cabin and we had plenty of firewood from old dry trees that belonged to Carl Poling. Sorry to say or tell you readers Carl got caught in combiner working by himself and that killed him. He worked us boys and paid us well only trouble we had working for him was the cross-breed dogs he had that would eat you up. We all had clubs to fight them off when we went to his place to work and he would say kill them all. Well, back to the cabin. The cabin we had fixed was nice and a place to cook our meals and we had plenty of foods like canned meats, pork, beans, and potatoes to cut up and cook in a big iron skillet. We could eat the same thing at home and it would be no comparison because it tastes so much better beside the river's edge. We had a lot of firewood and a lot of room to set our rods and reels and watched night trains go by and toot at us. One night our trot lines were all out and we all got lazy and didn't get enough firewood in to last the night and we let our lanterns run out of oil. Some of us were asleep in the cabin and some were asleep on the sand by the fire. Well, most everything had burned out and a cougar let out a scream behind our cabin and man did we all come awake with no lights, the fire was out, the boys outside were trying to get in the cabin and we ones inside were trying to get out, haha, we made a traffic jam in the doorway. I'm here to tell you we soon had our lanterns going and kicked the end of burned-off firewood back up on hot coals and had a fire going right off. I said to two or three of them, you guys take a flashlight and go behind our cabin and get larger wood to get more light around here, haha. They said, "No way, that's where that scream came from." All ten or so and me with a shotgun and flashlight all came back with arms full of firewood and that never happened again. We always had wood to last the whole night long. We all talked of what it was that let out that cry or scream and all agreed it was a cougar that smelled our leftover meat and unwashed pots and pans and skillet and none of us moving around came in maybe to have a meal with us all, leftover Spam, haha. When we were running low on food and pop we would jump in the riverboat and go to Sid Kapple's store for more canned food and soft drinks and charge it on Dad's and Mother's store account.

Not too bad of a living for us do you think? No bosses around and no work to do only look after our sand bar and cabin and swim in the river and just plain have a good time and free food not too bad for our gang and we three Huddy brothers. What great fun we were enjoying back in those days we loved the Hocking River sometimes in the evening the mosquitoes were trying to eat us up and we would put green willow branches on the fire for smoke and they didn't like smoke and would leave us alone. We could fish and stop slapping mosquitoes all evening. We had a lot of bumps on us from the bites. During the hot days at times, we spotted deer flies that could really sting or bite you and we would dive in the river and get wet and until we dried off they let us alone. We had to go home and catch up with our work so often that dad had lined up for us but in a few days or so back to our playgrounds and fishing cabin for more fun sometimes our uncles would come down to the curve and even our preacher that was holding a revival at the Church of God would come by and spend some time with us and take the boat for a ride and fish. He tried to keep us coming to services every evening. The Church had a baptism just below the river bridge and he baptized 30-35 young people while some of our buddies watched from the bridge. This area had a stone bottom and was about 4 feet deep and our older bro and sis would pray and sing to us. Then we would have a fire on the sand and have hot dogs, marshmallows, and pop. Good, great times for us all on a pleasant summer's evening. Around that time Dad and Mother sold our 5 acres up at Cross Road on Laurel Run Hill and bought Dow and Pauline's little home by Route 33. We boys made a shortcut path to our river curve about 5 or 6 hundred yards, across an old canal bed. Every now and then Mother would walk over to check on us and carry a message from Dad to come home and get it done. We may stay another week letting the grass grow and the garden weed in also, but we didn't want him to cut our food supply from Kapple's, haha. We also made homemade green fishing poles with 50-pound string and sinkers, and with green willow, we had plenty of them everywhere. While it was still green you could bend it almost double before breaking. I remember fishing in muddy waters in early March and it was cold and with big flakes of snow still coming down. If the river was too muddy and high we would go to the mouth of some creek to fish for suckers. The suckers would be going up the creek to lay their eggs and they were good and real sweet to eat. They had so many small bones though that we had to put them through a meat grinder, make them into fish patties, and fry them to make sure the bones were well done. We boys loved pan-size fish with flour, corn meal, and cooked in oil, like Rock Bass, Blue Gills, Catfish, Small Mouth Bass, and other fish. One of our buddies, Chet Wood, whose dad owned a riverboat and a big dog named Shep. That dog would swim behind the rowboat everywhere it went because it loved to swim, haha, it would not get out of the water until we came ashore. Shep also liked to get clubs and sticks we would toss out in the river and bring them back to us. He loved going to the river with us and he hated coons and killed everyone he saw. We had with us on our fishing trips most all of our buddies, around 10 to 12 of them, who would spend a night or two with the Huddy brothers. We would swim, fish, and mud fight. When we would mud fight we would get handfuls of old river mud and throw it at each other. It would stink and when you got hit in the eye from point blank, oh boy. We would dive in the river water and wash off and back to the mud and slime battle we would go, haha. We would try to wade and catch trapped fish in the backwaters and one of the biggest Small Mouth Bass I ever saw was around 5 pounds, we all just plain wore it out and he finally came up on his side and we put him on our stringer for keeps. We had car and truck inner tubes and would be floating down the river when someone would jump on you as you floated by and sink you. We would shoot groundhogs whose holes were along the river and have them to eat now and then. Not too bad tasting after you boil and fry them. We always had our old car parked near our campsite and could jump in it and go get some cold pop or ice cream at Uncle Ronald's Sohio station then get right back to camp because it only took ten to fifteen minutes at the most. We would buy a quart of Gem pop for 10 cents and drink it down because it got warm real fast along the river. We could pull up camp in a hurry when we got tired of it for a few days but it didn't take long to go back for a dip on a hot sunny day and hang around the camping area. We three Huddy boys and our buddies were burned dark brown from the hot sun and only wearing cut-off jeans for the day in case people would come by to see us and how things were going with us. Who knew what us three was up to back then you know as I get older now in life I look back on those days and really get into the good times we all had and now I'm trying to tell you younger ones all about our young lives from my memory. I know that Bob could probably add to these stories and Jim could have too if we had started it sooner. Sometimes when we ran our trot lines I remember our dad going with us and we took off 10 to 12 nice-size catfish, all over 5 pounds and as large as 10 pounds they were Blue Cats, Channel, Shovel Heads, and all kinds.

Fish brought home

We had a stringer full to take home and clean. We three boys sometimes wouldn't take our fishing worms off our hooks. We would just wind it up and put them next to the fence or one of Dad's buildings and our chickens would run loose and would see the fishing worm and down the hatch it would go. The chicken had a hook and pole dragging it around the yard. We didn't try to get the hook out but would just boil a kettle of water, kill her, and take off her feathers. We knew what was for dinner the next day. Dad would put up nails for us to lay our fishing poles up high and told us to take time to take the old worm off the hook when we were finished fishing that day. We would clean all the fish we had caught, bury our fish heads and other parts to keep cats and smell away then put our cleaned washed fish in salt water until we fried and ate them. Our sister Rona and mother loved fried fish and we had them a lot. They would fry them in a big skillet after dipping them in flour and cracker crumbs. Sometimes they put them in an egg batter and were they tasty.

Susan Huddy Blais

Indian artifacts

On our farm up at Haydenville or Stire's farm was one of the biggest Indian mounds in the valley and was right behind our one big barn and we boys were digging in it all the time to find flint and arrowheads. We weren't big enough to dig because it had berry vines and small trees on it and a real good place for groundhogs to dig their holes. I being a big-time trapper, haha, set up a big wooden rat trap and I checked it each day and had haywire tied or wired around a good-size tree, one afternoon I got home from school and checked my rat trap and would you believe it, I had a big groundhog caught by one of its back legs and every time I would try to pull it out it would growl and was mad at being trapped in the rat trap that was locked on just at the 13 joint. There was no way an old wood trap would hold a large hog and I was afraid to pull it all the way out because it might eat me up, haha. What a pair of choppers they have. I got Dad and took a ball bat and I pulled it out just so he could hit it in the head with a bat and what a big catch. Years ago, Indians lived on that land and we plowed in the spring and the soil was black then came the spring rain, and boy you could see flint arrowheads just by walking over the freshly plowed gardens. I also heard from history there was an army training camp of the Civil War in the field and every now and then a cannonball would be found by some farmer. The farm was right across old Route 33 and Wolfe Cemetery. It was two big old farms together owned by Fred and his brother Aurthur. As the years have rolled by the Hocking River has taken the biggest part of the farming land downstream and keeps on eating away. Fred and Aurthur have passed away and all older people up and down Laurel Run road are gone so that makes Bob and I the old ones now. You know any time you move away from the place you were raised and you come back later it seems like everything has changed. Now whenever I pass our old home place my thoughts take me back to years ago and the wheels start to turn again.

Iron bridge and cars

The old iron bridge we had a lot of good times on by crossing it in cars, and bikes, and Bob would climb up it to the top and walk across the river, up I would say, at least 50-60 feet above the river water. Not me, I'm a ground squirrel and stayed on the ground and let Bob climb. He was like a monkey and could climb tall trees and hang by his feet and even toes straight down nothing but hard earth under him I would chicken out and so would brother Jim and everyone in our gang. This is the same wood or plank floor that we had when we all had cars and later on, we would see who could cross it the fastest. I think our cars only hit one or two times and it was one lane and we had a flagman to tell us no cars were coming the other way so we would get speeds up to 60-70 miles per hour and hop or bounce across this bridge. I was driving Dad's 1936 Olds and I had Red Walter Baumgardner in the back seat to hold it down some and started at Price driveway, I got the green go sign, had it wound up, and jumped up on the bridge, and when the Olds hit the first jump our balanced back seat came up and Red almost broke his neck. He was a heavy-set boy and we could talk him into almost anything. The same bridge brother Jim had to stop on and the wheels locked up and he went through the guard rails nose first and landed on the front bumper. The rear wheels were up on the concrete and he had to climb down from the car. He saw Ralph VanBibber plowing his Dad's corn field and had him hook a chain to his car and pull it back up on the road and down the road he went. Ha

We three boys, cars, and the law

Jim, Bob, and I all ran like the law was after us on the highway and on gravel roads man. Dust, with 3 abreast on a country road, and one of us had to slow down because a one-car small cement bridge was coming up fast and our fenders and doors were bumping each side of our cars. Crazy and many times Nelsonville police would run us out of town to the end of the city limits and put Ohio Patrol on our tails but we had our feet to the metal and long up Laurel Run road and home before they came down Rt 33 to where we turned off. The police knew us and knew Dad and came to our home and told on us with jacked-up stories to really make us look bad to Dad and Mother. They would say to Dad, "Tom we're going to arrest your sons if we can find them." Dad asked them what we were doing to be in all this trouble. Well, Tom, first of all, they are always speeding up and down streets alleys, and around the square and burning tires on take-offs, second, they are running our red stop signs and third of all, they always have large crowds of young people around their cars on the square and we're going to get them you had better talk to them. So, Dad and Mother would ask us what all you boys are doing to make the law so mad at you? Nothing Dad they are sore because we give them something to do other than sitting around and eating donuts and coffee. I remember one night we all met at Busy Bee restaurant next to the newsstand in Nelsonville, we all had loud pipes and we parked always around the square and I remember most of us lived up Laurel Runway. Our 1st cousin Rudy Campbell lived up Campbell's Lane and we all had to come out of Nelsonville on Rt 33 or take to back roads like Lick Run Hill Road. We all saw the police car sneaking by looking at us in the restaurant and just waiting to catch us in the city. Our exhaust sounded like an airplane in a dive and was very illegal. I told Chet, Bob, Jim, and Rudy that they were going to write one of us up or put us in jail that night. It was after midnight and I told them to watch me because they wanted me bad. I was parked in front of Dew Hotel with the top down in a blue convertible 1941 pretty set of wheels, all blue lights, big red angel out on the nose. It had white flaps with blue lights, red and blue tail light lenses, and big hub caps that flashed when turning. I had loud thrush pipes on it and man I got in and cranked it up like a bomb going off and police were all lit up and I took off out of the town and Nelsonville cops started after me. I could hear Chet Wood crank his Chev. up and the cops took after him and about that time Bob cranked his 37 Chev. with a GMC truck engine in it and split pipes and manifold. He did it in front of the 10 cents store and was peeling out and Rudy Campbell was a Chev. Coupe and Jim were in his car and we were like ants going in every direction. The police didn't know who to try to catch and believe it or not we all cleared city limits and up 33 we all went we had them to the floor around 90 miles an hour and then all stopped and told our stories. We had the police confused with our loud pipes and burning rubber. Do you remember that time Bob? How about later on you and brother Jim had split manifolds and tailpipes, looked like two trumpets coming out from rear bumpers, and a state trooper had you pulled over and written you up for your loud pipes and brother Jim was trying to catch you before you got to Buchtel and came around the curve and had his pipes bellowing like a dive plane fighter and tried to quiet it down but too late Jim went by and trooper took after Jim told Bob to stay right there. He pulled Jim over. looked at his driver's license and said Huddy that's who I was writing up when you roared by, you know him? Jim said he's my brother Mr Trooper, haha, they were written up. What Bob and Jim did to their pipes I don't know. We all had pretty cars and on Saturday night the big night in Nelsonville and man it was a car show that every young boy wanted to show off his car around and around the square we would go tooting horns and wolf whistling, using fog horn bells and coon tails and extra chrome every place, curb finders and port a wall white side walls. Bob had one of the fastest 1937 Chevys in town I think it would hit 97 mph at best. It had a GMC Chev. truck engine in it and I believe he could outrun Chet Wood's 50 Chev. 6 cylinders. That would do nearly 100 mph. I had a 1941 Chev convertible that could outrun me. mine was for looks. One night Russ Barrows raced me and Lois with an Old V-8 1934 Ford and passed me like I was standing still so I sold it to Bob. He and Dad worked at Nye Chev. garage and I worked at a Ford garage. Fords and then Chev. came out with a short-stroke engine that was awesome and Old's had out an Old's 88-98 Rocket car and at the top end they could outrun a Harley bike 120-130 mph. I saw the Walker brothers from out of Pattonville come by our home on Rt 33 and you could hear that Old's coming with its 8 exhaust pipes coming out from under the rear. It had a wolf fog horn plus a set of musical blast horns. We lived on a long straight away and they came by 2 or 3 o'clock in the morning around 100 mph and blowing fog horns and a song of Yankee Doodle on the blast horns to let us know they were calling it a day. They were on the way home up the back of Haydenville where we made a dirt race track on their Dad's farm. Their dad worked with Bob at the Tile and Brick plant at the Diamond Plant. All in all, we had a lot of buddies who had hot cars, like Stub Turner, and Bill Siles one of the best wild drivers I ever rode with in his 1936 Plymouth. He would put that car in a spin on a gravel road and completely turn and go the other direction and dust, gravel, and motor going at the top speed. Bill could've been a driver for a dare-devil team, a big, easy-going boy from Haydenville. Chet Wood and I was up at Logan Street Fair and didn't have cars yet and we were thumbing for a ride to Logan way late or early morning and here comes Bill. We jumped in with him, and Stub Turner also from the little town of Haydenville, who had a 1938 V-8 Ford Convertible with a carload of buddies, the race was on to Haydenville and I was watching the big round speed odometer and said, I'll never forget it, floating power fast man back then, 6 cylinders. We went around 5 miles then there was a quick right-hand turn at the end of a long straight away and Turner was ahead because Bill picked us up. Bill said "Hold on I'm going to take him on this curve," the big long needle was on 85m.p.h. on the blacktop and Turner couldn't hold the Ford to the inside lane and drifted to the other lane. Buddy I never saw anything like it Bill had a big spinner on the steering wheel and passed Turner's Ford on that curve on the inside lane and laughed and he said "I knew I could take him there." Man, my heart was up in my throat. I saw a lot of good drivers including us 3 but he could handle that 36 Plymouth like a play toy. Others in and around Laurel Run like us were Denny and Rudy Campbell, Gene Sparks and Jack McQuaid, Page Martin and Dan Lightfoot, and on out by the fire tower Jessie White and Nelsonville boys.

Skating and that I couldn't

We were mostly up to the skating rink on the hill just out of Haydenville and it was a real hang-out back then for us, young girls and boys from all around our area or the other small towns down in Hocking Valley. My cousin Don Vollumer was the skate manager while hundreds of people were skating to the organ music of Ken Griffin like Pretty Red Wing. Don Vollumer could skate so well that it looked like he was just floating and hardly bent his knees and I couldn't stand up on skates at all. Bob was good and I think Jim could skate too. I remember renting the roller rink one night for $85.00 and the place was packed and I was going to learn how to skate if it hair-lipped me. I put on skates, and man you talk about a person being stiff, it was me. I was holding on to the wall and trying to make myself go, and along came brother Bob and his buddy from school Bill Robertson and they got on both sides of me, and away I went running on my back wheels trying to stay up. Now at the other end of the skating floor were the restrooms and it had a 2x4 rail in front of both restroom doors to catch skaters and stop them. These two got me going so fast and let go of me and I was helpless and back on my rear wheels. How fast I was going I don't know but I only saw the 2x4 railing right in front of the girl's restroom coming up fast. I grabbed the rail and right under it on my back feet through the swinging door of the woman's room. Some girls were standing there and said to me "Hey you're in the wrong restroom" and all the time I was crawling on my hands and knees trying to get out of there. My pride was hurt in front of the whole rink. I took off my skates and went to Nelsonville and let them all finish out the night. I saw more fights at that place than anything else with so many Army and Marines and service boys home on leave and finding their girlfriend dating some other guy and the fight was on. Good place to get your nose busted and eyes blacked. Not too much entertainment going on around Hocking Valley except the two drive-in movies, one at Athens and one across at the rink outside Haydenville. There were also

52

swimming pools at Logan and Nelsonville and free movies for three nights put on by Bob Row, two up from our Sohio and Shell stations. At Uncle Ronald's Sohio station, we also had a softball diamond or field, and man did he sell a lot of chips, pop, ice cream, and other foods at each movie night and we all had cars and a big crowd to watch old western outdated movies, haha, Mr. Row also had a free movie night at his place just outside the lower Nelsonville city gates and old Tom, Bob, and Jim were there.

Grandma Matty and the duck

I remember Grandma Matty we called her. She was a big heavy old woman I liked very much and she wanted me to help with her housework and to keep Grandpa Doodle away from her when he came home drunk. She had broken her hip twice and she was lonely and would give me some of her keep-sake things. She gave me a one-legged small yellow duck that rats or some other night predator got, that saw his little leg sticking down through chicken wire and bit it off. I felt sorry for the little thing because he couldn't keep up with the rest of the flock and had to sit and rest for a while and get up and hop along to try to keep up with his brother and sister ducks. I took the duck every place I went and he became a real pet by always being under your feet. I took him on one of Mildred's river trips and we put him in the river water for a swim and with only one leg he would swim in a circle. We had a lot of fun with him and all of our penned-up pets. For years after he grew to a big drake white duck and it hung around with our chickens and got so heavy he could hardly hop. I am sad to say we had a bad winter one year, the snow and ice were deep and he couldn't fight his way back to the barn and froze to death. We had wild animals penned up and also had groundhogs, an opossum mother, and 13 little ones in her pouch when we captured her when they were the size of small mice and we had a lot of fun. When we would put a swing rope up in an apple tree and put these 13 opossums on the rope they loved to climb over and under each other passing by. One day the head count came up short and we knew that one couldn't have gotten out so they kept coming up missing, one morning we saw her finishing off one of her little ones and someone told us to just let her out and go because she was lacking something in her diet. We had crows and even tried to get them to say a word or two but all they said was "caw". We let them fly away.

Harsh winter

There was a real bad winter and we were off of school for five weeks. It started with rain and freezing to the trees and everything and would bend them down to the ground. Then came deep snow on top of the ice and subzero weather and school couldn't keep classrooms warm even if the coal furnaces were on high, besides, our buses couldn't even think of getting to us on Laurel Run Hill. I didn't have to worry about electric lines or phone wires because no one had them up on that hill. All we had was coal heat and outside water and toilets and no one could get to us way up there. I remember Dad was off work and we had to resort to our cellar and home-canned foods to get by. One cold night it was snowing hard and a knock came to our front door and we wondered who was out on a night like that and way up here? We opened the door and there was John Norris, Chuck Wood, and Butch Baumgardner all of them had large crates with tops and had all kinds of food for us and carried it over a half mile in the deep snow because no one had seen us for a week or two and no one could get to us to help us with whatever we needed. Thank God yet for his help back then. They couldn't begin to get up the slick hill to us. What a gift from the Church of God that we went to, to help us out and those 3 men toting all that food to us on such a winter night. We three boys almost drove mother nuts upstairs playing basketball with the big balls of yarn rags and we would put friction tape around it to hold it tight and we couldn't do anything but slam dunk it or shoot it, haha, we had a homemade basket and she said get outside and play, so we would go outside and find something to do. Five weeks off school in the winter time and boy. Back then we didn't have to make up lost days because of the weather. Everyone suffered through it. Man, what a long vacation from school. We could slay ride from the top of the hill above us and turn downhill at the crossroads and start down the big hill and coast almost to Hocking River with not much traffic. The ice and snow got packed down well so we would take our sleds and do it all over again. We could belly smack on our flyaway sleds and go fast with a running start and get up to some fast speeds of I would say 30-40 miles per hour and our dogs were right after us, haha, so much fun we had racing each other and our buddies. Some winters Dad would not figure on enough of our coal supply and we had to cut dry wood with a crosscut two-man saw. We had our mule pulling a sled in deep snow as we boys would tear down old rail fences and cut them up in pieces to fit in our stoves and grate fireplace. The kitchen range needed wood also to cook with and to keep warm with and that was a hard chore. It would take 8-10 tons of lump coal to carry us through winter and sometimes we may have had an extra tough one and run out of coal and it was wood cutting, splitting, and hauling time anyway to just get by until spring.

Chores and work

We three boys sometimes had to wash out in the garage where mother and dad put an old hand ringer. We had two big wash tubs, a number 2 and a number 3. A large one to hold a lot of water which we heated water by the big kitchen range and when it got hot two of us would carry it out to the ringer stand and mother would put it in the wash soap. We had a hand washboard and a stomping clothes with a short handle and Mother had us three scrub and stumping clothes I did not like having to do washing on Saturdays. We and our buddies had something else we would liked to do every day but we always had our outdoor clothes lines, propped to hold the sagging lines of wet clothes from dragging on the ground. The sun did most of the drying and we used what seemed like 1000 of the long old-fashioned clothes pins to hang up our washing side by side. We three would try to get away from our house as soon as we could by just having breakfast and then taking off and getting lost. I remember one time we were mad about something we had to do from Dad's work list and Mother told us what it was he wanted us to do. We three were mad at each other over what tool we wanted to use and got into a 3 boy standoff. All of us were going to hit with some kind of tool and Mother heard us telling what we were going to do to each other and here she came with a long tree branch or switch and broke up the big stand-off. She told us to get busy on Dad's job. Dad always left a long list of jobs to do while we were on our summer vacation. Even if it was necessary like, I want them boys to take this lumber pile and stack it by the barn and make sure they put cross pieces crosswise to let the air through and won't warp. Just simple jobs to me but I'd say to myself, and mad, what's wrong with where it's stacked here? Dad would say to Mother get the boys to hoe and till the tree gardens. He would have a reason to go leave like Dow and Grandpa, and he had to look at a horse but mostly drink all day. It was all just stay away from us here and try to give us work to last us all day and I would want it done. Mother would keep right after us to get it done. Man, we had some things we wanted to do but that day was shot.

Anyway, we were into it when Dad started the big basement under our log house. All work was done by hard labor and an old scoop that weighed 200 pounds and we had to dig from out the side of the cabin and deal with a slope opening. We had to back old Kate down to drag the empty 200-pound scoop and one of us had Kate by the head and hit her in the face to get her to do it. The scoop had to go under the house to load by shovel and pick and take it out to a low place. The handle on the scoop had to be lifted to dump it and back to the house to do it all over again. To dig that big of a basement was a big, big job for us boys ages 13, 11, 10. It was cool under the house and hot out in the sun so that helped us out a lot. We were mad most of the day with all the work we had because it was tons and tons of dirt and digging and hauling out to dump it to build up the yard with filled dirt. Day in and day out, the same thing, man we were glad to get a day off now and then. I used to get mad and throw my shovel and say who in the world wants to make a living with a long-handled shovel anyway. Dad wasn't around near, and we three would be on edge and take it out on each other and Mother would hear us fussing and come down and say for us to use all that fuss on the job at hand. We got an early fall and we were still digging on dirt and Dad hung up old canvas to try to keep out the air and cold winter coming up in under the house and man what a cold house we had that winter. The wind would blow under the kitchen and come up under the wooden subflooring and our linoleum and upset our chairs. The basement job took 2 years altogether and when it was finished it was a really nice one. Man, what a job it turned out to be. Anyway, I'm still saying our dad worked us boys too hard while we were growing up like our buddies would walk or bike up to our place and want to go swim down the road on a hot summer day and there we were under the house digging. A little was okay sometimes but Dad had us three tied up a lot.

Susan Huddy Blais

Billy goats

One time an old friend was way up in years and he and Dad liked each other, he had a big team of billy goats with harnesses, a Steele-wheeled wagon, and a nanny female goat. When I said big I meant big. They had horns and the team of them together where almost as big as a team of ponies. He used them in his one-horse coal mine and they pulled out loaded cars with this big team of billy goats. He gave them to Dad and us, so we boys hitched up the wagon, grabbed a peanut butter and jelly sandwich and water, and headed out for the day. Anything just get away from home and take a long ax and hatchet and go to someone else's property and cut and build a log cabin in the woods there. No one cared or ever said or mentioned it to Dad. We cut and stacked the logs and put up sides with knot ends to keep the logs from rolling. Our team of goats was eating up all the leaves they could reach. At the end of the day we had eaten our jelly sandwiches and cakes up and as all growing boys starved to death we were right proud of our new cabin. It was many days of work so we and our team of goats were ready to head for home and the barn. Should have seen them hooked to the wagon and had harnesses just like a team of big horses. No picture of them, too bad. They were real billy goats and stunk like them too. I had to watch them all the time it was hard to keep them penned up because they could climb up and out of almost every place we would put them. I think I told of them getting loose and standing in our front porch swing while we were down the road at a 4-H meeting. We went home and locked them up but they had already done a lot of damage to our big apple trees and unwound bark from the bottom up as far as they could reach on their hind legs and loved to eat bark and most anything. A goat will eat all day long most anything too. We had so much fun with them and one morning brother Jim had made a homemade chariot out of a steel chair and put in two wooden shaves one on both sides of the goat and used an old poker for an axle and two garden marking row wheels. He had a goat hooked to it and looked pretty good letting the goat pull him around the house in the yard and he was right proud of his one goat cart. I wish we had a film in Mother's camera and got a picture of him. We all were out on the front porch watching him take his new homemade cart and one of the billy goats for a test drive and go up the hill with no problem at all. He started down the hill and sat like a king on his cart and forgot to put hold-back straps to keep the wagon or cart from coasting into its hind legs and scaring the goat. This happened and the big goat took off down the road in front of our place, Jim let out a war hoop and he happened to fall off his cart and got his foot caught in the chair. He lost his reins to the goat and we all looked and saw Jim being pulled downhill on his back and the big goat-headed for the house. We ran out to stop the goat and unhooked Jim's leg and he was real mad and shouting kill him, Dad, kill him. Jim's back was all scratched up and most of all his pride. We unhooked his homemade cart and put the cart in the barn. If Jim could've had something to hit and kill that goat he would've. Don't mean to laugh but it was a real show. He just plain lost it over his invention.

The new road

When the W.P.A. Program in the early 40s was putting people who needed help to work and Pres. Roosevelt came up with this program to put people back to work after the great depression. A new road was being put in coming up Laurel Run Hill and on by our home and all over the country. We three boys hung around with all these road workers and they took a liking to us and I would say a group of 50 men all working by hand with mattocks, picks, long-handled shovels and you talk about poor buddy, I've seen some of them have nothing but a dried homemade biscuit to eat for lunch and old patched up work clothes. They liked to talk to us three boys anytime during their workday they would work and talk to us at the same time. As I related in this story we had one deep well with good water and plenty of it. We would take their water can over to the well by the porch and keep them in good drinking water and it was hot that summer. Man did they like us boys fun and good fresh drinking water. None of them had any money so they would thank us by bringing little ducks and tame rabbits and other things from their homes. When the W.P.A. went on by our home there was this big cut-away sloped hill and big shade trees shading it and it was a real great place for us to play in the dirt. Mother let us wear short cut-off pants to play in and no tops so we were dark brown from the sun.

Our homemade fun and necessities. We three had to make our own fun, like we would make slingshots and use old rubber inner tubes that had good rubber in them back then. We made our own stilts, rubber guns, and corn cob darts with 3 chicken feathers stuck in one end of the cob and a spike nail in the other end of the cob. We would watch how high it would fly and come down and stick in the yard. We made parachutes with workmen's handkerchiefs and tied 4 corners with string and a bolt tap and heaved it way up in the air and watched it float to the ground. We made homemade toy cars and trucks used wooden checkers for wheels and a wood lathe for the body and nails to hold the wheels on. Made our own underground

62

crawl in the fox hole and put it under the garden dirt like a wooden tunnel and played army, haha. We would all climb up a nice-sized tree-like Hickory and bend it over and jump up and down like we were riding a horse. We made Indian bows and arrows, tomahawks, and rubber bands around our heads and stuck chicken feathers in it to look like we were Indians. We liked to play cowboy and Indian sometimes and had real cap guns and rolls of caps to play with, fun. When we got older and the 2nd World War was going on, a lot of things like rubber balls, and bikes were all going to our fighting men of the war. Food, like sugar and coffee, also went to the men so we would get ration stamps for each child for sugar, gas for our car, and no shotgun shells. If you could prove it, you may be able to buy a bike just to get to your place of work and use it as transportation to get to your job. You couldn't buy a rubber tire for any car and would have to patch leaks in the old ones with cold patches and use a recliner side tire made of string, to protect your tube so when you went someplace your car was bumping along, haha, like a bunny rabbit bum-pity bump. If Mother would run out of sugar before the month was over she would use Saccharine for coffee. We used post-um which tasted bad and it was made out of soybeans I think, it was bad tasting to us. Your everyday school shoes had to be repaired at home and we three boys had home haircuts, Mother did a pretty fair job on us with a pair of hand clippers, scissors, and comb. When we got a little older we didn't want our school buddies and friends to know our mother cut our hair at home. We would walk 6 miles to get it cut by an old man up in the shop at Haydenville for 25 cents a haircut. We had fun going and coming and doing a lot of boy things having to cross the bridge over the Hocking River. Price and Hattie had a small store back then and we could get a big Clark bar and cut it up in 3 pieces for a nickel, they had a lot of Indian arrowheads, spearheads, and tomahawks which we loved to see and ask questions about. I only wish I had some of them now. They sold us fresh strawberries in a big patch along the creek between the little candy store we called it and they knew and loved us. Everyone up and down knew us and loved to stop us and give us things to eat and visit with us. Great times and fun. We grew up with them, rode the same bus and went to the same school with them. Man, buddies. It might take us the biggest part of the day to go to Haydenville by the road and up the railroad for a haircut. Mother and Rona would cut up strawberries and bake homemade berry cakes and put milk and sugar on them and we boys also picked wild strawberries real sweet but smaller. Man, good eating treats. Now in the winter time, we had homemade ice cream the quick way or the long way. The quick way was to get a big kettle of fresh snow and back then it was fresh, with no pollution in the air like now, and put a can of milk, sugar, and vanilla and just take a large spoon and stir. You had what we called ice cream or the long way with the hand-churned crank, and was put in a container with whatever flavor you wanted to make and had chunks of ice on the outside making it cool and turning into good ice cream homemade, good boy, haha. Maybe over a slab of fresh homemade cake. I'm making myself hungry thinking and writing about this, haha. Mother had to bake or cook most of the time every meal and we all came to the table to eat and everything was passed around to us all and we were allowed to talk at the table just don't overdo it. Now I could tell you what our Saturday meal was going to be before Saturday got there. Good old cornbread and soup navy beans and we ate while the Buster Brown show was on the radio and had Froggy and Gremlin and his dog named Tag on our battery radio. Now on Sunday you could bet on chicken, noodles, mashed potatoes, or homemade meatloaf, haha, homemade cake or pies or Jello. We had a lot of lunches from our garden like radish, butter, and salt sandwiches with lettuce and we got by at school with the school meals that only cost 17 cents per child and 2 cents for 1/2 pt of milk. With no income sometimes, we wouldn't have the money so Mother did the best she could and packed our meals or lunches each day. Now I don't know if Bob remembers this or not but I do like it was yesterday. I took my peanut butter and jelly homemade bread to school wrapped in the Sears and Roebuck catalog because we did not have wax paper or tin foil back then. Then the paper would be held in place by some cord string tied around it. We didn't have buckets for lunch boxes like most children had with thermos bottles of something to drink. That my friend was because of no steady income at home to buy those things for us. Dad wouldn't keep a job so we made do. I love to think of the happy days we all had making our own fun. At Thanksgiving and all holidays, we made it fun by baking and cooking good food to eat. We had time off from school and not to worry about the school work the teachers sent home with us. Ha

Squirrel hunting season

The Hocking County Fair came in the fall and the schools would take off one day then so that we could all get in free and the cost of rides was low for school kids. The county band would play and march for everyone. Now that day was during squirrel hunting season and every one of our family even dad and mother went but not me, no way man. That's a hunting day all day long so I would stay home and stay in the woods and hunt. I loved hunting better than county fairs. I had my hot spots all over the woods near our house and man would I shoot the nut eaters. I love hunting season and would borrow a bike and at noon lunch I would peddle 7 miles home and then back out again just to hunt squirrels until dark. I would skin them and mother would bake home-baked biscuits called drop biscuits and boil and fry my kill and make gravy and we all loved that for a good meal.

Hunting

Well, I got sidetracked again with stories and my mind sorta' drifted off on something else. Like I keep telling our readers, these are my own stories and from my own mind. Brother Bob can add to it or maybe tell of some of the things I can't think of right off hand. Bob and I are the only ones still living and I'm sure he'd have more stories to tell of our hunting days. Now, next door to our place was old Tommy Cook whom I have written about, and old Emit Forest, his wife Minny, and a son called Buck. They were good neighbors and let us hunt on their property also. Across the road from us was an old cut-out drive through the trees and an old house not too bad of a place. We played some in it but it was a snakes den and we always looked it over before going in to play. No one lived in it for years so we would play army or use it as a fort. It had a lot of groundhog holes and blackberries and raspberries around it. Some member related to Matty named Laol Mazes bought it and hauled it away so there went our fort. Across the road in front of our house was the old Henry Todd place and it was loaded with blackberries and good woods to hunt. They would let us Huddy children hunt and play on it. It had a dug-out spring or pond we boys loved to play in or around and it wasn't too deep. It was full of crawdads, salamanders, frogs, and early spring peepers. and had water and leaves in it. Bob hunted some but I don't think Jim got into it like me. I would ride a bike all the way to Nelsonville when Dad and I would hear Carpenter's Hardware got a shipment of shotgun or rifle shells. When word got out old Tom Lee was there by walking on a bike. Shells were hard to get because of us being in World War ll. I saved my hunting license back as far as 1942 and I still have it. I put in a lot of hunting miles and hours and it was part of my life that I put in the woods and fields hunting.

I don't want to forget this story Brother Jim and I went rabbit and quail hunting down at Chauncey at Uncle Wiley and Aunt Ivalou's big farm and unloaded our guns, got our hunting coats on, and loaded our shotguns and walked between the big cattle barn and old pig pen

67

and wouldn't you know it, out jumped a big fat rabbit and caught us off guard. I had a 410 shotgun and got off a quick shot, put another shell in the chamber, and put on the safety and the rabbit was just kicking around and wasn't going anywhere. At that moment I had done a foolish thing and I knew better but I put the stock of the shotgun on the rabbit's neck and the gun went off. The shot hit my hunting cap, blew its cap bill off and the heat burned my forehead and that's how close I came to shooting my head off. Brother Jim reminded me of that just before he passed on a while back. He said, "Man that was close, Tom. You shot your hunting cap off your head on that cold, frosty, winter morning. Only God was watching over me."

We had a lot of stories from our hunting days, here are a few more. I was hunting one day by the oil well pumping rigs and the motor was back firing every now and then and the sound was like a shotgun going off with a loud bang. I saw a bunch of young squirrels and I shot one and the other squirrels never ran or paid any mind to my gun. I don't know my count that day but they were used to the oil well motor backfiring. I would see a squirrel another time and shoot it and I would hit two of them with one shot. Two in one shot, good hunt. Never got bitten by one but they could eat you up after being shot and not dying yet. I had to make sure he was dead before putting him in the back of my hunting vest or coat. I had one come too and it was jumping around at the base of the hickory tree and I put my foot on him but he sunk his sharp front teeth all the way through my boot and just missed my big toe.

One clear fall day it was very dry and I was trying to sneak up on a squirrel and I got in shotgun range. I shot and hurt it and it was jumping around and I was in a hurry to go pick it up because it was making a lot of noise. All of a sudden, a big red-tail hawk came from nowhere, grabbed my kill, and flew away with it. I shot the hawk and took him home, spread his wings out and I had that for years with a wing span of maybe 2 1/2 feet.

One day I was hunting, and most of the time I was alone hunter, I shot this squirrel and he fell at the foot of the tree so I marked the tree and just sat still because I was in a good spot. I would shoot my limit of squirrels, go and pick them up, take them to the car, and put them in the trunk. This one day out of nowhere came a big black dog and went right to the tree and picked up my kill and away he trotted. Strange thing, I say, I don't believe in strange signs never did or warnings like a lot of people I know do.

I did not believe stories that some people would tell and get myself spooked out but as a young boy I had to walk from Route 33 to the top of the hill after dark, all alone and I wouldn't let my mind get spooked out. I hated to walk over Hocking River because of the wooden plank flooring that would beat to your walk and steps would shake the whole bridge and you would come up on a real dark spot where trees hung over the road and the bridge was rattling and you seem to be making a lot of noise. What worried me was we had cougars running wild and loose all around us because of the timber wooded areas and rocks and also livestock like young pigs and sheep and other helpless ones.

After I got out of the Marine Corp. in early 1954 I hunted only for a cougar that people had seen and even my old grandpa Doodle Huddy saw it and heard it splashing up the small Laurel Run creek. The creek had stone walls on both sides of it and his dog who whipped about everything up and down in the area barked one night, Grandpa opened the door and Rex the dog was backing indoors. Grandpa could hear it splashing up the creek in the water. Then he had a big flat roof garage dug back in the hill and it sounded like a person walking around on it and also Grandpa would throw his trash and leftover food up over the tile wall that held the hillside back. One night he went out to throw away something and a big cougar growled and ran up over the hill. I wanted to shoot it and I had a Browning automatic 12-gage shotgun, and I stalked it for a long way in the woods and up and down the hills and dales and never got a shot at it.

69

When I would get close to it, it would let out a cry and run and keep out ahead of me and it knew I was after it. Mother kept telling me not to go to the woods alone but, no not me, I was a big strong marine. My Uncle Dow was working at Natco Brick Plant at Diamond and had the big door open and was just sitting eating lunch and something moved at the edge of the parking lot and road. It had big white pines along the way and a couple hundred yards away a big cougar walked out of the pines and gave him a look. He must have been in that area and smelled Uncle's lunch. Don't need to have lunch with a big cat. While on the stories of cougars, when I was 17, and as I have said, I was a lone hunter. This late fall I drove up to a hill about 3 miles from where we lived on a little place on Route 33 and it was Lime Bank Hill to us all. Our school bus climbed it 5 days a week taking us to school. Right on the very top of the main road was a mud logging road and people also dumped trash because no one could see you unloading. There were a lot of sneaky people back then. Just drive back in a wagon road and dump trash on your land as if they owned it. With my old car, I went way back to the end of the road and parked it. I walked down an old 3-C boy's path made back in the 30s and it was so dry and at the bottom of the path was a creek that followed along Laurel Run creek into the Hocking River. I was squirrel hunting and stayed in the wet, damp running creek to save on noise from dry fallen leaves on the ground. It was quiet down in the hollow and I found a good log to sit on, all at once I heard the breaking of tree limbs and it sounded just like a person fell out of a tree and thud hit the ground behind me. The first thing I thought of was a cougar or black bear watching me and I couldn't see for all the brush so I took off, and man I could run like an Indian, back down the creek to where the path made its way up to the car and I stopped a second to hear that thing coming splashing down the creek after me. I ran my best to reach the car and all the time thinking he would catch me before I got in the car. For years I wondered what was after me and one day hunters were telling hunting stories and Cy Lanning who was Zoeta's husband told us that a cougar had run him from the woods up on Lime Bank Hill while hunting. I could say about the same time I got run out of there.

Back when we both were on the Union Furnace Warriors basketball team in the 40s, our bus got back to the schoolhouse around 1:00 in the early morning because the whole team stopped up in Logan for a snack. That made us somewhat late getting started for home and I remember it was a very cold winter night and our only way home at the top of Laurel Run Hill was walking about a seven-mile hike. With our handbags off we started up along Simple Creek and there were a few homes along the creek. We turned and headed up this long old hill we called Loomis Hill because old Nub Loomis lived there and had a saw mill there. We were moving along at a fast pace wanting to get home and get warm from the cold moonlight night and around zero temperature. It was wooded by the timber trees on both sides of the road and the trees were snapping from the cold and you could hear every noise in the woods. We stopped to get our breaths and there was some noise from down in the deep wooded hollow on our right, I asked Bob "Did you hear that?" and he said "Let's hit it" so off up the hill we ran and he was a head of me because he was much faster then. If a big mountain lion, or we called them cougars, could run about 40-50 miles per hour it wouldn't do me any good to try to outrun one. Bob joked and said, "It would've gotten old Tom first and give me time to get home." After a long burst of speed, we had to slow down or stop and try to listen but only heard our own breathing and hearts beating. Anyways, drivers had said more than once they had seen cougars crossing the road at night before we had that walk on that long cold night. Down at the Diamond Brick town, Ed Norman had his young pigs eaten up by one. Other stories came up from the other time of sightings of big cats and black bears around our area. We both got spooked at that time and were glad to get home where our mother was waiting for us to get home.

My dad saw a mother and two small cubs run across the road and into the cornfield where we boys camped a lot of times. I loved to squirrel hunt and this was a story later on in life, that I and two buddies Ed Roush and Tom Dishong went down near Lake Hope in Wayne National Forest down near 2 miles. It was called Zelaski. I went up a creek left of the logging road, late that afternoon, I had stayed too long and darkness caught me. I was way up in the creek hollow with my water canteen on my hip and it was a real warm September afternoon and I headed back. I was making my way back down the creek, sawmill road, and the old wooden bridge that was partly rotten with age, and I stopped to get my breath. I listened to every sound around me in that area and then I heard this stomping and growling. I thought it was one of my hunting buddies stomping mud off his boots and clearing his throat so I yelled "Hey Tom, Hey Ed." I didn't want one of them to take a potshot at me making noise coming up to the bridge and old logging road. There was no one around though and I had a quarter of a mile of hiking yet to get back up to the car. When I got to where we had parked I asked them "How long have you two been waiting for me?" and they said "Nearly an hour" I said, "There must be someone hunting down by the old bridge." We went home and never thought anything more about it. Tom's brother wanted to go down to the same place to hunt because we all got our limit plus. We told him where to go and the next day off he went hunting and made his way down to the old bridge and was standing on it when he heard a growl, at first, he thought it must be a bull or cow in the woods and he looked down the creek where I had been the night before. There was a big mother black bear standing up on her hind legs and letting out another growl. He said he was so dumbfounded that he yelled "A bear!" The bear started after him with her two cubs and he ran as hard as he could just knowing she could grab him from behind before getting in the car and ended up bending his door key trying to get it unlocked. He couldn't wait to tell us about this and we went all together to look for her and sure enough she had a den near the bridge, it was an old slab pile. She didn't like me coming by the night before and was warning me to get out of her area. Me and my brother-in-law Tom Dishong both had 12 gage Browning shotguns so we wanted to make a black bear rug of her and if the law caught us we'd still be in prison. We had it all planned and the guns had 7 shots as fast as we could squeeze the trigger. I've heard how hard it was to kill an enraged bear. Me and Tom had our killing slugs and guns in the car and stopped for a morning snack and coffee at a restaurant. Tom was saying that we both had 14 shots together and could kill any bears that we came across but old me read a bear story where four men got almost eaten alive after wounding a bear. I almost chickened out and I told Tom just what if one of our shotguns failed to fire only leaving us with one gun and seven shots at an enraged mother bear and two cubs she was guarding. I asked him "Is a bear rug worth it?" We called it off and went squirrel hunting and think it was a good call. Don't you? Ha

Dad's Cougar Story

While we are on wild cougar stories let me tell you one that our dad told us children that happened to him when he was a young man. He, Grandpa Doodle, and Dow lived on old Wolf Farm back in the twenties and Dad worked and helped farm. He also had a job at Nelsonville's East Clayton Brick yard and had to walk 4 miles on an underbrush path near Lick Run Hill along Hocking River back and forth to work. He had to leave the house before daylight and, back then, used a miner's hat and carbide lamp with a big reflector to cast out a big light ahead. He said he was making his way along the path and river one morning when all of a sudden, a big cougar screamed like a woman getting killed and jumped down on the path in front of him. He said he didn't know why it didn't come after him but it could have been because of the bright light he had on his hat. He said his hair stood up on the back of his neck the rest of the way to work. This was told to us Huddy boys when we were young. Here is a story of one of my best old friends who did a lot of welding for me he, was from a sawmill town in West Virginia. He lived way up in a hollow between two hills and had a mud road that led to the main highway with a creek that ran along the road. There was an old rail fence between the road and the creek. He said he was 17-18 years old and got a job in a small town and his dad's birthday was coming up so he had laid him away a 38-caliber revolver and 2-3 boxes of shells. He took a bus back to the end of his home mud road and had the new gun. It was almost dark and he said to himself "I'll just load this thing up and maybe I'll see something to shoot at." He had a flashlight too and it was aways to walk to his house and a lot of cougars had been seen in this area. Anyway, he started to walk, and over on the hillside a cougar let out a scream so he picked up his pace. He said this cat was stocking him and wanted him bad. It kept pace with him, growling all the time and jumping in the creek water and splashing up the creek in pace with him so he knew it was out to attack him. He stopped and had the new gun in his hand ready and this big cat came up and started over the rail fence, he had a light on him and he emptied the 38 calibers on it at almost point blank. The cougar fell back on the other side of the rail fence and he wasn't about to go and see how it was. He went home and told his dad what happened and his dad said they would go down the road in the morning to see if he hit it. They went down the road and on the other side of the wooden rail fence was a big cougar so they called the game warden and law and told the story. They showed the law the big cat and they wanted to put him in jail for shooting a cougar out of season. Can't win them all. What if he hadn't had that gun with him that night? Man…

Country Boys vs City Boys

The barn war and bloody eye:

I remember one time our dad's aunt or cousin and husband came to Uncle Dow and Pauline's home and invited Dad and us three brothers over. They had 4 city boys our age and of course, no one paid us any attention because they couldn't let that cold beer get warm so they told us to go play and find something to do. Then back they would go to their loud stories, laughter, and talking up a storm with a couple of cold beers to make the jokes flow. All of us boys went down to the barn and started to throw corn cobs. Bob, Jim, and I were outside the old barn and we ran the four Athens city boys inside the barn. They ran out of corn cobs and started to use old dried-up horse droppings, hard as rocks, and not to be outdone we went to gravel and rocks off the county road that went by the barn. They would open the barn door and try to hit us and close it again. One of them, the second oldest, was looking out of a crack and telling them how or when to blast us with hard horse pills. I and Jim were getting a new hand full of rocks and Bob was peppering the side of the barn near the door. The city boy that was peeking out wore real thick glasses that looked like the bottoms of coke bottles and our Bob sailed a rock into a crack and hit him right in his right eye lens. He let out an Indian scream and even his mother Gail Johnston came running down to the barn with her husband and saw blood coming out of his eye so off to Athens hospital they raced with him screaming at the top of his voice along with his mother and dad. Uncle Dow was so mad at us and it was one of the closest times Dad ever came to beating us. Hospital doctors took 18 pieces of glass from his eye and it took a while to heal but those city cousins knew better than to start wild fights with us three Huddy boys up at the crossroads at the top of Laurel Run Hill. Mother and Dad would say to me "Look after your two brothers and I did. I went after anyone that was going to beat one of them up. Then Bob was about my size but I was a little broader and heavier than

Bob and Jim was a year younger. I was a year and a half older than Bob and I was one and 1/2 years younger than Rona.

Carp trapped in the field:

The Hocking River water overflowed into the corn fields and then when it started to go down some of it would get trapped in the field and man the big carp were everywhere. They had no way to get back in the river so us with pitch forks would carp hunt and jab them with our forks and some would weigh 20- 30 pounds. Haha, fun.

More river stories

Now our Uncle James Huddy, dad's youngest brother who lived in the town of Nelsonville had a nice cabin on the Muskingum River below Stockport Ohio and we boys helped him work or build a new one later. He would come up to our place and give us, at the time, 10 cents a piece for big soft craws and hellgrammites for his use in Mus kingdom river. We would sieve Hocking River ripples and peppermint patches and get some real nice bait for him. Two of us would hold a 6 to 8-foot sign in the ripples and swift water while 3 or 4 of us with old tennis shoes on would move and scuff rocks in the swift water. When the soon-to-be bait were knocked loose from rocks and stones the swift water would carry them into our side and we would raise up ourselves and we'd have crayfish and hellgrammites and large river minnows crawling in it and we would just put them in a big bait bucket. He would come up to get and pay us for them all. Haha, we were always in the bait business and used all the leftovers for our own trotlines. We also hunted for those large bullfrogs at night, that bellowed like a foghorn and you would have to see one to believe it. It had legs the size of a hen chicken and we loved eating frog legs and frying them in our big iron skillet with fish and fish eggs, haha, good! I have to say here that we killed some big river snakes too! We tied our hooks for snapper and leather backs on our lines that were tied to large willows with old spoiled meat dangling in the water which was a good way to catch them. We saw some big ones in our day and our Uncle Charley and Millard Patton had some that would almost cover a No2 wash tub and may weigh 20 pounds or so. Also, we saw some good-sized catfish maybe 22-25 pounds but nothing like the size that Brother Bob catches in the big Ohio River to this day. One of the biggest smallmouth bass we boys got was out of a back hole after the river had gone down. It was trapped and we boys saw him and just wore him plain out, if I remember he weighed over 5 pounds and that was a good size smallmouth back then. Later, Bob had a motorboat and was coming in for a landing and a good-sized bass jumped right into his boat, haha. We had a carp on trot line one morning and I had the large line in my hand and I believe Bob had the oar and we were downriver below the sand bar and I could see him and tried to get the rowboat so Bob could use a gaff hook on him. I just couldn't believe the size of that carp. The river water was clear and it was the biggest one I'd ever seen in my day. That carp weighed 50 pounds easily and we had our hooks all baited with locust that year because it was I guess 17 years time and they had been eating up our trees, singing all day long, falling in the river, and drowning. The fish was having a field day on them. So, we would just hook 4 or 5 on a hook and drop it back in the water. Have you ever seen them every 17 years and watched them everywhere? We also used worms that were called catalpa worms and would also use them for bait. Nellie, Harvey Wend and grandma Campbell-Brown had their trees loaded. We boys would go pick up cans full of them because the fish loved them. One year a big tree came down river in a flood and wedged behind a big rock and sycamore tree where we tied our river boat. The tree reached all the way to the sand bar because it was so big. We played King of the Log with our gang along with Uncle Pete Taylor. We would push each other into the river until the last one standing was the King of the Log. The tree lay in the water half under and you could walk all the way across to the sand bar to fish and it finally washed on the down river in another high-water flood. All the river floods took away a lot of our river fun in due time and years. The curve is still there and to us, it always will be the curve. We also made homemade boats and when they got water-soaked you could hardly row them. It was the wrong kind of wood usually because we used old oak boards. In one river flood, one of our boards broke loose and we found its way down near Diamond in a driftwood pile. There was no way to carry the board back to the camp site so we got it up on the steel rails of the train tracks and pulled it up the track. It was hard work but we all pushed and pulled it back to where it broke loose from our cabin and it was not really worth it at all. To get our worms to use all we had to do was dig in the old corn fodder at the end of the corn field. The corn fodder washed in at the end of the river's high-water edge and man you could get a can full in a hurry of red worms. Our nightcrawlers would catch in Grandma's big yard after dark with flashlights and put them in a worm keep box and kept them damp for weeks and months.

Moving and my license:

Mother and Dad tried to sell the highway home and I quit school in 10th grade, that is when we all moved to Uncle Wiley Ryan's farm where Aunt Iva Lou and her children lived in a big farmhouse. Up past the farmhouse was a small house that we rented for part of a summer and a long cold winter. Dad got ill with a bad stomach ulcer at that time and Bob stayed with the Ryan's while he was in 11th grade to finish out the school year. We moved partway up Laurel Run Hill in the old Wiggin's place and we stayed there until Dad and Mother traded the small house by RT 33 to a woman and children who wanted to get out of Nelsonville city. Dad traded places to move on Adams Street and I got a job at Natco Tile Plant at Haydenville firing kilns for $1.21 per hour and paying mother and dad for room and board in Nelsonville. I was only 17, had my driver's license, and worked the second and third shifts at the time. I paid Mother and Dad $40.00 per week. I must also tell of the time that Bob used my driver's license while I slept and had a wreck downtown Nelsonville, gave the police my license, and got away with it, haha. I went to the wreck and everyone was calling him Tom and me Bob, haha. I got my driver's license in 1946 in Logan and had no problem passing my test because I had been driving for years. When I was 11 years old I drove on Route 33 and with me was a lot of buddies too, haha. Everyone would pitch in change for gas and it only cost 17 cents per gallon back then. We would all ride afternoons on Sunday in Dad's old cars and homemade trucks. We three Huddy boys could hardly wait for spring to come so we could go to the river and fish.

Mushroom picking:

We, boys, would also go mushroom picking and loved those big corn cob ones. I remember one spring when the river water was up high near the small airport at Diamond and when the water went back down a big patch of them came up every place. People would just pick them up, put them in their pickup truck beds loose, and come up out of the fields with a truck load. Man, I never saw that happen again in time. Now, I've got into patches of them and picked and taken them home because we all loved them. We had a lot of meals from out of our cellar and gardens.

Fights among we Huddly brothers

We three boys were the caretakers of the gardens and our family had 3 big ones to hoe and harvest when the time was right. Mother and Dad would let brother Jim off the hook, as most younger siblings were when work was to be done. Jim would play with bugs and not keep up or even try to hoe his row or do his part. Bob and I would tell Mother to make Jim work along with us and Mother would say to leave him alone he is the baby of the family. We would say to her, then get him out of the garden so we don't have to watch him not working like the two of us. She would call him into the cool house with Rona and let them off work and play. Bob and I were mad about them getting everything and we had all the work to do and that made us mad over almost anything so we would fight each other. Our buddies would come by and want to go to the creek swimming hole and we couldn't go because of our gardens and farm chores dad would leave us to do that day. There seemed to always be a long list of things for us to work on. That was old Dad. He and I never saw eye to eye about things and had trouble in our lives about it later on. One morning we were hoeing our big gardens and the girls that live up the road came 6 days a week to get their mail from a row of mailboxes. It was the end of the mail line and their box was next to ours on a long board. The girls had crushes on us boys and always found something to talk about and kill time away from home. They wanted the apples on an apple tree next to the garden we were hoeing. The girls saw them a way up in the top of the tree and wanted us to knock them down, so us good old boys started throwing hard clods and anything we could to bring them down and I was looking for a piece of 2 x 4 to heave up in the tree. Old brother Bob heaved one up and hit an apple limb and it came down and hit me in my hairy head and the blood was coming out and I was half knocked out. I ended up beating Bob in front of all the girls and Jim went for the house to get mother to stop the fight. Jim told his mother that I was dragging Bob all over the garden and his mother came and broke it up. That was years ago but until this day Bob will say it wasn't so bad getting beat up but it was in front of his girlfriend.

Tommy Cook

Our good friend and neighbor Mr. Tommy Cook loved to stop at the fork of the road at the top of Laurel Run Hill to give his horses a break after a long hard pull up the hill where we three Huddy brothers lived. Mr. Tommy Cook lived by himself above our place in a cave naturally made and had good fresh spring water coming up from an underground spring. Tommy used it to drink and cook with and it was real good soft water. Over the cave he had put a small building to keep his supplies so Tommy would every week like clockwork hook up his horse to an old high wheeled buggy and go to Nelsonville to shop for food and go by way of Lick Run Hill down to town which was Nelsonville Ohio and a trip to this town was a good 10 miles or so and when he would come home he came up route 33 to our Laurel Run Road and come up the hill by our place and he loved to talk with us three boys very much while his horse rested and we always had a lot to tell him and he chewed Redman and Mail Pouch chewing tobacco and spit every so often and had this big red dog named Shep and he was never on a chain as I knew of. Mean dog if he didn't know you. It went every place he and the horse and buggy would go. It was a mean dog to other cats and dogs along the way. Well, old Tommy would pay us three boys for helping on his farm or place and gave us I think 50 cents per hour and always paid us at the end of the day. He would give us things from his place like ripe plums and grapes and wild bee honey that he cut and took from a bee tree and talked about sweet and in long bee combs and he gave us some times chicken eggs because he had a lot of laying hens around all the time and had a lot of sweet corn and green beans. One Saturday about noon we three Huddy boys all had Red Ryder B-B guns Daisey lever action and 500 shot and we got good at aiming and shooting anything that moved, we could shoot down big butterflies and even bumble bees around our flowers and Tommy asked if our guns could kill mice and rats and we've already done that before around our barn. Old Tommy's place was next to our place and Emmet Forest's place and we all got along well. Tommy later on let our 4-H softball team use his hay field for a ball field. We told Tommy we could kill mice and rats and he asked if we wanted to make a little money shooting them at his barn and we were all for that because we liked anything to shoot at. We told him we were out of B-BS and he gave us some money and said get some and come on out to my place and you can shoot as long as you can. Mother let us three roll an old rubber tire each way and take off toward Coonville about seven miles away to a mine-owned company store and they had everything for what you needed. We could get good brass B-BS then 500 per box for 10 cents a box so back home we started rolling our old tires and stopped to take a swim dip in a cold creek and threw rocks and boy things. We had school buddies who wanted us to stop and play. We got home and got ready for the next day of shooting had plenty of B-BS and were ready to shoot. The next morning a hot summer day we took off to Tommy's place and opened an old gate to the old horse mud or dirt road back to the rear of his home in the cave and old Shep let him know we were coming and Tommy came out and said now boys I'll put my horse in the stall and feed it as I do and when I put corn in the feed box you can see for yourself to believe it. The horse would try to eat and mice and rats would bite it on the nose when they heard Tommy putting corn nubbins in the box. Tommy took the horse back out of the barn and we started shooting as fast as we could and mice and rats fell every place. We had 500 shots each and more B-BS with us and again you should have seen us shooting mice and rates everywhere, we shot for a long time until they stopped coming out of the dens and holes and it was so late in the afternoon old Tommy paid us three for our slaying of the most mice and rats I have ever seen in one barn. What a field day for us. Now a little more to the story about Tommy. I was told by older people who knew Tommy that he had had a nervous breakdown when he was a young man that scarred him for the rest of his life. The story was that Tommy and his buddies went rabbit hunting in their tween ages and his shotgun went off and killed his best buddy, he never got over it and Tommy got married and had children our ages and older and went to school with us at Union Furnace. I knew two of his sons one was my age, his name was Bernard. I was told their home got on fire and burned down and Tommy and his wife parted and he went to live in the cave like a hermit and wanted to be alone. Tommy liked us three boys I would say because he missed his children and was lonely. In the fall of the same year, Tommy cut his corn with a corn knife and the fodder shock rubbed his neck while cutting and shocking it. One day he stopped by on the way from Nelsonville and I noticed a big old red handkerchief around his neck, I asked him why he was covered with an old handkerchief and he showed me and it looked bad to me and I told him he had better see a doctor about it soon because he had gotten poison ivy in it and had a bad looking neck and he went on home and later died from I hear blood poisoning and someone found him in his cave dead. Man. Too bad we lost a good old friend and missed him coming and talking to us three. I never did know what ever happened to his horse, farm tools, and land because Mother and Dad sold our 5 acres and home too.

Dad

I'm not trying to pick on Dad in my story but he was the main trouble in our family because of his work record and driving problems we all had to suffer at very young ages while at home. I don't know how many jobs he lost, or how many times he would move mother and us kids from place to place, school to school. He never once came to watch me play a game of basketball, football, or anything else. He didn't seem to care whether we had a ride or any money to get to our games. We tried to take Mother and Rona to a game in an old Ford Coupe and Bob and Jim would sit out in the cold in the rumble seat on a sub-zero night and cover up wrapped in blankets. We had to let water out of the radiator to keep it from freezing up and fill it back up after the game. Our school boys pushed it to get it started because the battery was no good and we ran off a generator after the motor got going. Until this day I have a hurt in my heart about that. I still believe that if Mother had passed away Dad would have let someone else raise us. Bob may or may not agree here with me but it was the way I saw it and still do. We would go to away games with not a cent to our names. The team would stop for hamburgers or such and someone would say to the coach "The Huddy boys are still on the bus". The coach would come out and say come on in boys and I will buy for you. It is sad to say but it was very embarrassing. This is only my side of the story and Jim's or Bob's may be different. I remember being the last one in class to get my money, 74 cents, for a workbook in grade 3 or 4 grade and for a month or more the teacher would say "Tommy, when is your mother or dad going to send the money for your workbook"? "you are getting so behind". I would tell my teacher day after day that I would ask for the money again. We would be the last ones to be able to pay for our school pictures and I remember when the whole school had a Hollywood picture show in the gym and it only cost each student 10 cents to see it and I along with real poor Coonville kids had to go to a classroom and study with a teacher watching over all because dad and mother couldn't round up 4 dimes for us four again. Mother gets my vote for making it through as we did. Dad never told any of us three boys, I love you, son, just when I came back from Japan and had been for one year, I got no hug just a handshake. Sad, sad, sad. Sorry readers I still have a void yet in my heart for a father figure and I will have it until I die. This is me and my life story just letting you know my feelings. Our dad would quit his job in the middle of the winter maybe not liking his foreman or boss and being out of work for a long time, it made it hard for us and Mother to get by. Well, you can tell from this book dad and I never got along well at all and had a lot of tension between us. Sad, yes, my main thing was just to get away from him and the no-pay jobs he wanted us to do so when Uncle Pete Taylor and Aunt Flo came to our home we'd ask them to take us home for a week or so. I am sure they let on like they needed us to help on their farm and take us back with them and they sure showed us a good time. They would take us to Buckeye Lake Park to fish, overnight, to the movies, boat rides, and things we weren't used to and Dad got a week drinking spree at home. Mother would take Rona, leave him at home, and stay with her mother Grandma Campbell, and Mildred or someone. She would then write Flo a letter asking her to keep us for another week until she and Dad got things patched up then when they were back together we'd come back. Sad, I say. Happened so many times, over and over hard on us four children going from school to school like when his dad Doodle Dow Sr. had dad along with his brother Dow JR help him farm again. They moved us up near Haydenville across Rt 33 and Wolfe Cemetery and the Stire's Farm which had a large river, corn fields, and two old farms together. Grandpa Doodle again was a big boss and had some Nelsonville buddies who were crooks with money and decided to put in a lot of crops and Grandpa Doodle had all the tools and machinery to work with. We sided in with the cash feed store and we cut up 3 tons of seed potatoes to plant. We boys worked and got off school for 50 cents an hour to help put them in along with a large field of watermelons. Grandpa Doodle, Dad, and Fred Stire used a lot of us young boys for cheap labor. The summer went by and harvest time came along and you never saw so many spuds being plowed up and lying on top of the ground. Our backs got so tired of picking up potatoes at the end the of day we could hardly straighten up. The pay of 50 cents per hour was a lot of money back then during the 2nd Star World War around 1944-45 and most of the older men were called to fight. We younger boys were called upon to help out a lot at home. They took small trucks of potatoes from that farm and here is what happened to most of the watermelons. See, down from our barns were the big fields and they had a farm road all the way to the river from Rt. 33 highway and across the highway a company had a row of homes for poor employers to live in. A lot of boys like to fish in the Hocking River and use the tractor road to go to the river as a shortcut. They weren't bothering anything, just crossing Fred Stire's farm and old Fred stopped them and told them to walk around his farm and to not trespass again. They had to walk to the end of his farm to reach the river and that caused a heated fuss between them. There were acres of melons ready to pick and ship to the market and a short time after the fuss seemed over with them using the road. Fred went to check on the melons and found the whole field of melons were punched, cut, and turned over so he couldn't see it until they were turned over. We wondered how long it took those boys to punk all the melons at night and I'm saying in my story I guess he should have let the boys go ahead and use the farm road. Anyways, Fred blamed them for breaking window glasses out of the 2nd old farm that no one lived in for years and I heard some of those boys spent time in BIS up in Lancaster Ohio for busting glass insulators from the telephone poles. Maybe they had it coming after all and some of them were a little older than we were. Our bus wouldn't pick us up unless we walked down to Laurel Run Road or we had to go to Logan School because we lived on the line so to speak. We could go to Eighter School and we were already well into the year at Union Furnace School so we would walk 1/2 mile along Railroad track morning and afternoon or highway Rt 33. Mother kept us along the rails when she could then a few years later the school bus came up to the line and picked up the school kids. Always a dollar late and a dollar short. Our home up at Crossroads on Laurel Run Hill was still empty and for sale. Mother was fed up with our farm life and on one Saturday Dad was out drinking with Brother Dow Jr and Grandpa Doodle. I said I wanted to move back up on the crossroads today and the only way to move was by a buck board wagon and our mule Kate. We had three boys, Rudy, Denny, Zeta, Rona, and Mother. We moved everything back to the crossroads and it took two days to load and haul and we would go by our friend's house each time. It was summer and we must've looked like the Beverly Hillbillies going up Laurel Run Road with our belongings all tied on the mule wagon and heading back where we should have stayed in the first place. When Doodle, Dow, and Dad got home our grandma Mattie was still living on part of the farmhouse and Dad asked "Where is Nell, Rona, and the boys" Mattie said, "She moved back to Laurel Run Hill home." As usual, a few days later, Mother and Dad were back together again. I'm trying to tell you readers about some of my life's hard times that I remember. It may not be interesting to you but there may be some of you that want to dig deeper into our home lives so I'm putting it in my book. Dad had a job at a strip mine company later on after we moved back to Crossroads and he had to drive over to Carbon Dale Town where he was in charge of pumping big water backup holes. Workers could get to a vein of coal and Dad tried to keep out the water as best he could. It was zero out one night and we parked the old Ford car at the top of the driveway because it had a no good battery, never had a good one. I remember we would get it started and it would run off a generator and keep the motor running. Well, it so happened that somehow the headlight bulbs were burned out and he had a long way to go on the old back gravel roads with no lights. He and Mother dressed me as warm as possible and I sat on the front fender with my feet on the front bumper with gloves on and I held a coal oil lantern up so Dad could see the road. I was holding on to the burned-out headlight with the other hand and we went about, I would say, 13 miles and I almost froze to death. Man, and when we got there the mining workers had 55-gallon drums and a pile of slabs to burn to keep our hands warm and dried out the wet gloves and socks but the pumpers and the smoke would almost put your eyes out. When daybreak came we got the old Ford started and drove on home because now we could see anyways but we had no heater at all, now I say that's part of hard times. Wouldn't you? Now again these are my memories and no one else's and I went through these hard times and it still sticks with me today. Everything was the hard way but we made it fun in our own ways and are still here yet today. Yes, Dad would let me take the old car everywhere in my younger years which was great with a carload of buddies, Bob and Jim. I remember one time we were way out from home and the gas fuel pump went out on the old car and we Huddy boys had to come up with some way to get gas to carburetor. We took a plug from the gas tank, filled a pop bottle and an oil squirt can that we put gas in. Then we put up the hood and Bob sat on the fender and squirted gas into the carburetor to keep it going until we got all the way home. Another time we had an old model Coupe with a lot of our buddies along because they pitched in on the gas and I didn't have my driver's license yet. We were on the hill and an old man who was on crutches hobbled across the road in front of his house and with me coming down this steep hill with no brakes, the Lord was with us. I went between him and his mailbox and almost ran him over but it did knock him down. Thank you, Lord. I learned to drive my grandpa's tractor and then moved on to an old truck and then a car. I drove my mother to the store up Route 33 at the age of 11-13 years old. One day I was driving an old homemade truck on a gravel road when the freezing rain started to make the gravel slick and the truck went into a tailspin, we went three times and Mother was yelling all the time at me to get it to stop. I did get the truck to stop and never even left the road and I ended up still headed the way were going. When she went to Nelsonville to shop she later made sure I was along to drive us home in case Dad wasn't able to drive us. As soon as Mother and Dad got to the town of Nelsonville city Mother and Rona went food shopping, Dad took off to the beer-drinking bars and we had to find him. In the short time it took Mother and Rona to shop for the food, Dad would get loaded and not able to walk or drive us home so Mother would let me drive up Lick Run Road the back way to get home. Sorry to say but we would have to leave Dad at the bar and they would get him home at closing time. These were some of the hard times we were put through back then. The only time I can remember Dad ever taking his family someplace was after a drunken spell and he would put us all in the old car or truck and take us for a ride to make up with Mother for the way he had acted. I don't even want to think of those things but it's still locked in my head. From the time I was 17, we had trouble seeing alike with each other and it never ironed itself out. I don't believe Dad ever took any of us three sons in his arms and hugged us or told us he loved us. Not even when I hadn't seen him for two years, I only got a handshake from him. Oh well, I will get off that thought in my story. Please, readers, remember, that it is my life story from my younger years, from memory.

World War II and Uncle Paul Campbell

World War Two 12-7-41 Uncle Paul Campbell my tenth birthday

Uncle Paul Campbell was on my mother's side of the family. There were different stories about how he escaped from the Germans but those were not true. One such story was that a Russian woman ran a truck through the prison wire and broke it down and that is how he got away. This is the true story right from Uncle Paul Campbell's mouth. Then World War II started on my tenth birthday and I will never forget it. I remember that Sunday morning at about 11 AM or 12 noon and we came outside of our Church of God down at Laurel Run Road called the Locks Church of God near where my mother and grandma Nettie Campbell lived. All the people were talking that the Japanese had attacked us and bombed some of our big battleships in Pearle harbor. I asked my mother on the way home at the top of the hill and across the road where we lived, "Mom, they won't take me in the army will they"? She said to me "No Tommy you are too young yet to go". All we heard on the radio for a few years was that Hitler had large youth armies and with my age in it and that is the reason I asked her. It took most of my uncles and a lot of them had to go and fight for our good old U.S.A. because Uncle Sam needed a lot of our young men. The uncles that had to go were, Uncle Paul Campbell, his brother Foster, Uncle Pete, Ralph Taylor, and brother James Huddy, and a lot of young men were drafted all around our area. I will tell you some things my dad and I have seen and stories they told when they were home on leave or from being a P.O.W. in Germany. My uncle Paul was missing in action for a long time and no one knew if he was killed or a P.O.W. in Germany. Then one day a soldier wrote his mom who lived up above grandma's home in Haydenville to tell her that he was a POW also and told her to get in touch with Nettie Campbell because he saw Paul and he was alive and well. Uncle Paul was unable to write home to his mother as of yet. Now when Uncle Paul came home for good we were all there to welcome him back and he told how he was captured and we all were all ears and questions.

Later on, in my teens, I asked him a lot of questions because I was real proud of him because he endured two and a half years as a prisoner of war and had a lot to tell us. He was captured by Rommel's army in North Africa. Here is the story he told me. His rifle group was dug in the fox holes in the hot desert and watching a German highway with a lot of German trucks and tanks going past where he was dug in and they only had light fighting guns. All was quiet and they were just watching the German army pass by. Along came an Arab trying to steal a field jacket from one of his fighting buddies and was caught and spanked for it. They were dug in about 500 yards from the highway sand road, the Germans were using which had tanks, half-tracks, and large guns. They saw this Arab that tried to steal the field jacket and stopped a German half-track truck, it was pointing at us who were dug in and the Germans didn't know we were there. They didn't know we were there watching their every move so close. We only had small weapons like army rifles and hand grenades when here they came with big tanks and we had nothing to stop them at all so we had to wave a white flag and give up. There was a German officer who went to school at Wisconsin University USA and told us just what to do and they knew what to ask us as they took us as P.O.W.s. I was put in a barbed wire compound next to the Russian P.O.W. compound and found that the Germans did not like the Russians at all. Uncle Paul got to get messages home to Grandma and us all, that he was alive and a POW, and that way Mrs. Bond from Haydenville heard from her son too. That is when he told his mother to call the Athens messenger to put the whole story in that paper. The Russians were starving to death and the German guards tried to get Russians to come out of the tin hut and would hit the hut with clubs to get them outside of it. The Germans would send in police dogs to chase out the Russians but the Russians would kill the dogs and eat them raw. They had no food so they had to eat the dogs because they were starving. Now back at home, Grandma sent Red Cross care packages ten pounds at a time and I helped pack them to help out because the Red Cross was allowed to go to the prisons to give our P.O.W.s his packet. Back at camp when the Germans found out Uncle Paul was a farmer and knew he could grow vegetables he was put in charge of work farms to help grow crops for the German armies. That is the way he spent most of his two and a half years as overseer for the gardens. The Russian army and American Army were closing in on the Germans and their camps with us in them so we were made to go on a P.O.W. march to keep us ahead of both armies. They had guards on both sides of every 16th person and 4 rows of P.O.W.S. Now if a POW couldn't keep up with the march and fell out a German century would run him through with his bayonet and leave them dying along the old country road and keep us moving with one small drink a day and one potato. When we slept at night they would bed us down in some old barn and we slept on the old hay until daybreak and they would make us form ranks and away we would march for another day just to keep us moving. We could hear the big long-range guns firing coming after the Germans who were marching us fast to get away and going nowhere. That night we were bedded down in a big barn of hay and I was plain tired of not going no place, when darkness came I dug myself down deep in the hay and when morning came the centuries would jab their bayonets in the hay but I was down so far in the hay they didn't reach me so off they marched not missing me. Around noon I was sure they were gone for good and I got up from my hole hiding place to my surprise not only I had hidden there in the barn of hay but around 10 to 12 of us made ourselves free men once more. This German farm was run by 5 or 6 German women while their husbands were away in the German Army. They were afraid of us at first because they were told the Americans were mean to the women so they finally came around and started to fix nice meals for us and good farm food like milk, eggs, and fresh baked bread for us. I started to fatten up some from the 125 pounds I had become and pretty far from the 200 pounds I started with. We POW men were free alright but in the wrong country and we knew we had to get back with the American army some way and keep out of sight of any German troops that may still be around this part of the country and would shoot us if they caught us because we had nothing to fight with. We were just hoping for the American troops or Russians to come along and turn us over to the Red Cross. That day came while we were having a good cooked breakfast one morning and all of a sudden, the kitchen door was kicked open and two mean American troopers had us looking down the barrel of their guns. We all said we are American P.O.W.s so don't shoot. We all were happy to be back on the right side again so we thanked the farm women for the good care of us and were turned over to the Red Cross. Uncle Paul looked pretty good by the time he was released to come home for good. I was always proud of Uncle Paul because of all he had gone through during the Second World War. When Uncle Paul was home for a short time he married Nellie Mae Pearson from Logan Ohio about 11 miles from where he lived with grandma and his mother. After their wedding, they stayed at Grandma's to help take care of her house and got a team of workhorses to work with. Uncle Paul helped us boys dam up the creek and make a deep hole to swim in, it was cold creek water but wasn't too bad after we got used to it. He let me drive his old blue 1934 Ford and we would drive over to Lake Hope about 20 miles away and take Nellie Mae along to fish for some big bluegills, also Paul and Aunt Nellie Mae would play in Grandma's yard many games of the ball we had a lot of fun with them. When I played football for Nelsonville, Paul and Aunt Nellie came to watch me play and more or less encouraged me to keep playing ball because my own dad never came to watch me from my recollection play ball at either Nelsonville or Union Furnace schools. Paul and Nellie Mae came to Harper Hollow Street to live just a few houses up the street from our home and I helped Paul and Nellie fix up the new home. I hauled Brick from up at Natco Brick Factory where he worked. I was in tenth grade at the time and I could drive and help. Now after Paul and Nellie Mae had their baby girl named Evelyn I would sometimes babysit her so they could go to the movies and have an evening off to have a good time. I didn't mind taking care of her at all. Aunt Flo and Uncle Pete owned a farm out from

Logan and Paul and Nellie Mae moved in with them after a while and helped out with farming and so on. They and Uncle Ralph, Pete and Flo, and Paul and Nellie decided to move to Columbus and look for jobs and get away from farming for a while. They made new mobile homes or trailers in the big barn where they lived and did a good job on their new homes. When the trailers were finished they headed for the big city of Columbus to work and live. Uncle Pete went to work at a machine shop across the street from the trailer court and Aunt Flo went to work at the big department store called Lazarus and Uncle Paul went to work as a clerk at a new Cousin and Ferns store on Main Street down the street from where they lived. Paul and Nellie Mae later moved to a smaller town called Warsaw Ohio and Uncle Paul was crippled with arthritis from the hard life as a POW laying out in the open weather all cold and damp in Germany. He was so crippled in his legs and feet and in so much pain all the time he could hardly walk and get around. He took painkillers each day and one hot day he was cutting his yard grass and had a heart attack and I lost a good Uncle. Uncle Paul had Evelyn who lives here in Newark and has a set of twin girls. Also, Aunt Nellie Mae and Uncle Paul had 2 sons, one who passed on and one who is still living.

World War II and Uncle Jim

Uncle Paul Campbell, Uncle Foster his brother, Uncle Jim Huddy, Dad's brother, and a lot more young men had to go. Uncle Jim was my dad's youngest brother and had a schoolteacher wife named Lena. He was my wife Lois's teacher in the grade school of Doanville where Lois was raised. Everyone loved my Aunt Lena because she was a good woman to everyone and Lois loved her too while in grade school, not knowing that one day Lois would marry into the Huddy family, small world isn't it? My uncle Jim was a heavy equipment mechanic and worked for a large mining company in Kimberly Ohio near Nelsonville with Aunt Lena working. Also, had no children they had a real nice home but the Navy Sea Bees needed him so it was. He fought the Japanese overseas in Soloman and Gautam Canal and other islands in World War 11. He could operate a dozer, grader, shovel, and all heavy equipment and made air runways for our planes to land with supplies, food, and so on. He told us many a time he would have to jump off the dozer and get under it because of a surprise attack. It was what he called hedge hopping with the Japanese zeros that would fly just over the tree tops to get a sneak attack on him and to delay the building of a new runway. Uncle Jim said the streaking bullets would just zing off the dozer. The Sea Bees came to a shore after the Marines hit the island a day or two before and there were dead bodies everywhere, both Japanese and our Marine Corp. men that had been shot, and Uncle Jim would take the dozer and dig graves and just push the dead into the holes and cover them up. He would also push Japanese bodies off into the sea and let the surf and waves carry them out to sea. Also, dogs and cats would fight over dead bodies before he could get them buried in the sand. Uncle Jim's ship went back home after his service time and was sent up to Alaska to finish his time out of the Sea Bees. Then back into Nelsonville and back into coal mining. He and his wife Lena never had any children of their own. They would come and get us three and pay us for helping them build or restore a fishing cabin down on the

Muskingum River near Stockport and we hauled a lot of brick from where I worked. They bought new brick through me because of my discount by working at Natco and I got them for 3 cents a piece at that time Bob, Jim, and I loaded a tow pickup truck and made a run every day in the summer to build a new brick cabin to enjoy in the summer time. We had river boats with motors and would go up the river to a lock and dam across Muskingum River called Luke Chute Dam. The river had locks and dams every 20 miles apart to control water flow so we knew the river behind their brick cabin real well because of boating, fishing, and staying with them all weekend. Uncle Jim on my father's side was good to us boys and took us hunting and fishing a lot while growing up. He told me if I had done well in high school football he and Lena would send me to the O.U. College to play for the Bobcat at Athens. I stopped going to school in the 10th grade and went to work. Smart guy, I was then. Our Uncle Jim died because of smoking and losing his lungs and Aunt Lena died at home doing housework.

Bob and I are at the sports

The Todd brothers had boys our age and size and every year Don was in Bob's room and would say to Bob, "At the end of summer vacation I bet Harold can whip Tom this year". He was way bigger than me. Bob would say "I wouldn't put any money on it because Tom's been doing a lot of practicing on me all summer". Bob and I got into a lot of fistfights through the years over almost anything and with his quick temper and me wanting to knock it out of him. Haha, he would say after a fistfight with me "You cotton picker, you're not getting away with that". I loved him even when his nose was bleeding. Our Buddies would wait until our battle was over or keep saying "Come on guys stop fighting and play ball". Bob could outjump me in basketball rebounding but I had sharp elbows and on my way up or down I would hit him in the side of his head. Bob could also outrun me with his speed and I could run over almost all the line and break into the clear and I could hear him coming on me but sometimes by the time he slid down around my legs, I may have run 10-20 yards for T.D. Brother Jim was a little younger and smaller and some of the other players too, just half-hearted tackling. Bob and I meant business with each other. We took the ball team everywhere to play other sandlot teams we were hard to beat with Bob running outside and me blasting through the middle of the line and we had a big line with Rudy Campbell and Walter Red Baumgardner and Chet all weighed over 200 pounds and we went up to Haydenville one Sunday afternoon and beat Logan Highs team most of them from Haydenville going to Logan school and Bob had a hurt leg and could hardly run but I kept pounding the middle of their line. Then we went to Doanville Town where Lois and the Tingers were raised up and we met our match that day. The boys were mean like us and all sizes and most of them were married and out of school and had on baseball cleats to play us in that game. We came out of the game with broken noses and cuts from baseball cleats and fist-fighting with them. Man. Hard to beat.

The Old Todd Farm

One day in the summer before the Todd Farm burned down we saw this big old water barrel that was left by the oil well company and man was it large. It had old grease and tar pitch all over it and was leaning and tipping toward the big hollow long ways to the creek and it weighed a good two tons so we boys wanted to see it roll down the hillside just for the fun of it. It was leaning anyways so we cut some pry poles and all three of us put our poles under the back side of it and it had been sitting there for years and we all 3 got on the end of our pry poles and rocked it and tilted that big wooden barrel over and you should have seen it go like a big wheel down over the long hill. It smashed in the creek and bank then collapsed and the big steel bands that held it together came off and it was just a big pile of lumber laying in the creek and it had flattened over all the trees on the way down the hill. We kept that quiet from everyone. Later on, we told Chuck Wood about the stock of a good-treated pile of wood lying down in Todd's hollow. We told them it must have just rolled on its own and busted up when it hit the creek bank. He and Chet Wood, his son, took and dragged all that wood up to the road with a horse and put a new floor in his barn. It was free wood and we never told anyone of rolling it over the hill. Now in my story, I saved old Henry Todd and his wife from burning to death in the old farmhouse one day. I went upstairs to a bedroom where they went to die together and the house was a torch with thick smoke. My class school friend Harold Todd happened to stay home from school the same day I did and he and his dad and mother lived across from his old grandma and grandpa. He saw the smoke coming up from their old home and no one was home at his place. He tried to get them to come out and they ran upstairs and wouldn't come down. There were no phones yet in that area so he ran to our place crying and shouting for help. It so happened when his grandparents were first married they had hardships like the rest of us back then. I was out of the doors and I looked and a cloud of smoke was going up in the sky and man, I could run back then and Harold was a heavy boy and said his grandpa and grandma ran upstairs and he couldn't take the smoke. I reached the porch opened the door and a lot of smoke met me so I took the wet wool sock and held it over my nose and could hear the old ones calling for help. Then I made my way up the stairway with my eyes burning. I found them and told them to hold hands and hold onto me and I got them out and the house was a torch. It was a mud lane back to his house and I was almost done in by the smoke. I think I was 14 or 15 years old so here came more help and little by little help started to arrive, they had bottled gas tanks in the back of the house and they went off like a bomb. The house burned down fast and the roof slate had fallen in before the Nelsonville fire truck got there. The Todd's had a large family and all thanked me for going into that burning house and talking and leading them out or they would've burned to death. They were both up I would say in their nineties and could hardly walk and I was pulling them out. He led them to his dad's home a short ways down a mud lane and made them stay in and not look at their old home place going up in smoke and fire. Butch Baumgardner lived down the road from our grandpa Doodle and had a carload of men coming to help with the fire. At the same time my Grandpa Doodle was watering his team of horses which were unsnapped from the stalls and the horses would, just on their own, walk across the road to get a drink and walk back over to the barn and Grandpa Doodle never had to lead them. Here comes Butch's big Olds who ran fast to get to the fire and ran into one of my grandpa Huddy's big horses. It kicked out his grill and radiator and smashed in the hood and the big horse weighed a ton and made a wreck of Butch's big Olds. Nothing much but a scratched-up leg happened to the horse, haha. Grandpa Huddy came out of the barn a cussin' Butch for not watching for the horse crossing sign. I don't know what ever came of that deal. I know that Butch and Grandpa were mad at each other for a long time. The Old Todd Farm was across the road from our place, at the Cross Roads, and across from Tommy Cook's land and farm. It had two hollows going down from it and a brushy pasture field where we picked many gallons of big blackberries and man I mean lard cans of them big patches everywhere and they told us to pick and help ourselves to all we wanted and allowed me to squirrel and rabbit hunt on their place. I spent many hours hunting on Todd's farm in the woods.

High School band spoof

I was out of school and working and I was pretty thin in size then 17-18 years old and a big contest at Nelsonville's football field for a Halloween parade and judges and any kind of act to be voted on for prizes. Aunt Mildred and Zoeta Campbell talked us boys into putting on a show at this contest. Zoeta still had her drum majorette set of clothes she wore when she was at Nelsonville High School and even her old white boots and everything fit me. They also talked us boys, Red Baumgardner, who played bass horn, Fred Wade who was snare drummer, Jim, and Ralph Sparks, and a lot of Union Furnace band members with their drums and horns into an act. We had two cars or maybe three to get us to Nelsonville High School with our small marching band. We knew to sneak into town and walk to the football field that was packed that night. From out of nowhere here comes this put-together marching band of ours. I was trying to strut and couldn't twirl the baton at all but I could point to my band and people were stunned. They had big wagons as stages and I took our small band up to the end of the football field. Our drum beater was really getting with it and as I went under the goal post I gave a big blow on my whistle and down the field we came about fifteen of us trying to march to the drum beat. Guess who was out in front of us doing cartwheels and all kinds of moves, our brother Bob, and he was dressed like a clown, haha. We all came down to the front of the stands and the people loved it and here our big base drum said "Union Furnace Marching Band". To this day it's a wonder we didn't get in trouble with our school, I had on a red eye mask and a wig and no one knew who we all were until we blasted away when the contest went on and old Bob won the funniest clown and with us playing and cheering him on.

What a great time while we were young. Aunt Mildred and Zeta who helped talk us boys into it had a lot of love for us all. Rudy, Fred Wade, Ralph Sparks, Bob, Jim, Walter Baumgardner, Chet Wood, Jim White, and I made up our band and put on a play that night. So much fun. If only we had a camera or something to take pictures of that one. Nelsonville paper did have Bob's winning clown picture and name in it.

1931 Desoto and other car stories

Mr. Edward Fisher and his wife Nelle lived between Mr. Harvey Wend and his wife Nellie Alison and Campbell's Lane. The Fishers went to The Church Of God on Laurel Run Road and loved us boys and all the children near them. They had no children of their own so Ed had a nice field for us boys to play football and loved to just talk to us and have us boys around. We always had a lot of buddies playing at our place at the time we were living with Grandma Campbell. There were boys our age coming out of the woods by bikes from Haydenville, Nelsonville, Doanville, Floodwood, and Union Furnace. Union Furnace is where Lois's family the Tigners lived. Groups of teams would try to beat us there in Campbell's Lane field and we were tough to beat at times. I had brother Bob in the backfield along with me as a fullback and Red Walter Baumgardner at 240 pounds, Rudy Campbell our cousin also over 200 pounds along with brother Jim, Ralph Sparks, Fred Wade, Chet Wood, and other boys from around our area, and the rougher the better, we loved it. Ed Fisher and his wife decided to trade the old Desoto for a new Ford in Nelsonville. Dad knew Ed well and found out about the trade on cars so he talked to the salesman at Ford garage about getting his first chance at that old wheeled 1931 Desoto. The salesman let Dad have it for the price of $127.00 and make payments on it for $18.00 per month. I had my driver's license by that time at the age of 16 in 1946 and Dad told us if we could make payments, it was ours. Now what fun. I can tell you a lot of stories about that car so here goes. There was always a big crowd when the Huddy boys were coming to town and it always looked like a fight on the town square with young girls and boys ganging around us. There were carloads of us country boys. Nelsonville Police didn't like that at all. They wanted to put us in jail so bad. Our buddies would park near us and the crowd got larger. When we had the old spoke-wheeled 1931 Desoto we painted it from all black to two-tone blue with red wheels all done with paint brushes. We had big raccoon tails hanging down from the radio antenna and all slicked up. Sometimes, the paint was still tacky and had hayseed and dry straw sticking in it yet and really not dry enough to be driving around. We had to get it in the car parade around the square and ring our bells and wolf whistles and hit the fog horns with our big hub caps and mud flaps. There were blue lights hanging down and a big woman angel out on the nose of the hood that lit up. What good times. First of all, Ed Fisher had it from new and it was a 1931 Desoto made by the Chrysler Company. It was a 6-cylinder and it only had 31,000 miles on it because Ed and Nellie only went to Logan and Nelsonville with it once or twice a week to shop. The car was all mohair inside and the seats were like new with window blinds that pulled up and down so the sun wouldn't hit you in the face or someplace. It had no heater and no turn signals at all back then and a spare tire wheel on the rear end of it. We kept gas and oil in it and all of our buddies were helping put in gas back then. We three Huddy Brothers owned it as long as we kept the payments up on it by cutting grass and mowing the old winding cemetery Road. That is what we did to keep up the $18.00 per month payments. We kept the roads hot and went to the city of Nelsonville and everyone knew us from all around 3 counties or so and we always had a carload of our buddies with us. We were a pretty loud bunch of noise makers with tooting all kinds of horns, doorbells, wolf whistles, and fog horns. Then we would have a lot of fun driving back and forth just past Nelsonville where we lived, then back to Laurel Run, Wolfe Basin, and to Haydenville and that was five miles up Route 33 out of Nelsonville to our place. That is why the city kids knew us so well because we went to school there.

One time on Saturday morning we wanted to change our colors on the old Desoto so went to Cables Hardware and got battleship Navy gray paint, thinner, some paint brushes, and rollers. We also got some dark blue for the four fenders and silver for the wooden spoke wheels. Finally, we all were painting and don't you know it the summer rain came so we knew we had to put it inside somewhere, we put it in Chuck Wood's barn and the moisture in the air just wasn't going to dry the thick paint job. While we were waiting some of our smart buddies decided to go up in the loft to play in the hay and made the hayseed and small chaff come down all over our wet car so it looked like it was tarred and feathered. We still took it to town with a gray body and blue fenders and all the hayseed still sticking to the wet paint and our signs, wet paint don't touch.

We were in Nelsonville one Saturday evening and as usual, I had a car full of brothers and buddies and was coming up by Bert Tolliver's home. I didn't even know my wife-to-be was there working for Bert, her uncle. Here we came with some of my buddy's feet and legs sticking out of the old painted-up Desoto and shouting and pounding on the sides of the car doors and having a good old hello Nelsonville here we are. Her uncle Bert took a look at us as we passed his house and he, Lois, and her aunt Wilma were sitting on the front porch enjoying a nice summer's Eve and here we came. Bert told Lois and Wilma "That driver should be arrested and put in jail" and Lois agreed with him that they had never seen or heard so much racket in all her days at her aunt and uncle's home in Nelsonville. At the time their daughter Ruth Ann was running with Brother Jim. Lois's future husband was the driver of that old car and all that noise. If she would've known it I doubt if she would've ever dated me later on. She told me later on that she would see that old car parked at one of my girlfriends in Nelsonville. Later on one evening, I was on the way to a Union Furnace basketball game and it was snowing big wet flakes of snow, my windshield wipers back then were run off the vacuum from the manifold and it was a poor setup back in 1931. The windshield was a straight piece of glass and the snow was building up on the wiper blades and wasn't wiping the snow off. I must have hit the glass too hard to clear it and out popped the whole glass windshield. It slid out over the hood and radiator and under the car and I ran over it and it busted in a million pieces. The wet snow just came in and plastered your face, haha. Well, it was hard to find a 1931 window glass we went on using the old car all winter long and let the winter weather hit us in the face. We used heavy blankets to try to keep warm and I even took some of my girlfriends on a date and it was like riding in a convertible with the top down. They loved it because it was so different to go down the road with the snow and rain hitting you head-on. When spring came around we still were without a windshield and the state troopers were starting road checks on the cars. One day Bob, Jim, and I were up at Uncle Ronald's Sohio station and someone told us they set up a road check going into Nelsonville so with no windshield we took the back way to where we lived at the time on Adams Street. We got to Nelsonville and was near the High School and saw a lot of kids and bikes in the street and we said it must be that someone got hit on a bike. The city policeman stepped out in front of us, flagged us to a stop, and said to me this is a road check Huddy on that old car you're driving. He started a checklist with lights and tires and he got to the windshield wipers that were just hanging there and said to me turn on your wipers so I did. Man, it was swinging back and forth and he reached over to see how good the rubber on the blade was and that's when he said "Hey you don't have a windshield in this car you know that Huddy"? I said "I do know that" and he said, "It's illegal to drive without a windshield to protect you from getting hit in the eyes or face with something, did you know that Huddy"? I said "Yes I've heard of that before somewhere" and he gave me a list of things to be fixed or take this thing off the streets and have us look at it up at the police city hall you have 48 hours to get all these things fixed and get a safety check for the window Don't let us stop you again or off to jail you will go, Mr. Huddy. They just loved us. We couldn't find a windshield for it so we had Barney Neman, cut us out one from plate glass and put it in for $13.00 and we went to the city Hall and got a sticker for it. Would you believe we drove that old car around with just plain window glass and that would cut your head off if ever you were in a wreck with that window glass right in your face? At that time, I was working up at Natco Tile Plant as a kiln fireman and on the third shift, when I went to bed for rest Bob would take my driver's license and billfold and take the old Desoto downtown. He would drive around with a carload of buddies and we were the same size and looked somewhat like each other. One morning he was in a 3-car wreck on the square and gave them my license and told them he was Tom Lee Huddy, the police believed it and we sweat that one out until the case was all over and cleared.

One night I was running too fast on a gravel country road and had a carload of buddies with me and I could half see ahead of me with the old headlights. I went into a spin and how many times we turned around and around I don't know. Only God was with us that night and we never went off the road, man. Another time we were pulling our rabbit cages in a trailer down near Doanville near Circle Hill and we had this big pen with our 4-H project rabbits. There was a tall one so we slid it in the homemade trailer and we hit some bad places in the road Route 33 and don't you know it just fell over. Some of the rabbits got out so we ran them down and reloaded our cage and on down to Ryan's Farm we went.

Bob, Jim, and I had a sow pig in a hog crate taking her to our Uncle's place to have her breed, and in a ton, the cage door slid open and was a flatbed truck and there were no side rails at all. Somehow that hog got walking around on the truck bed and wanting to jump off the truck and cars were coming at us waving to us and we boys would wave back. We happened to look in our mirror and saw that hog and our hearts almost stopped. We pulled off slowly, got up on the truck bed, opened the crate door, and pushed her back into the cage.

Now by the time I did meet Lois, I had a job up in Columbus and had a real pretty 1941 Chevy convertible, Robin egg blue and all the fancies lights, mud flaps-angel that lighted up out on the nose, and blue lights underneath it and in the grill. It had blue tail light lenses in the rear, big flashing hub caps that belonged to brother Bob, and a new white convertible top. There were new leopard seat covers, a gold dash, and two spinners with pretty girls in them, a real eye-catcher. Along with wolf horns, fog horns, spotlights, doorbells, loud thrush mufflers, two tailpipes coming out from under the back bumper, and a zip-up bug catcher on the front grill plus fog lights. A real car, a show wagon. The Nelsonville girls would want a ride in it with the top down and we would say no it's too cold in March and buddy they would climb over the sides of it and get in the back seat unwanted and wanted a ride out of town. I told brother Bob to turn on the heater and sit up close to the dash and windshield and I put my foot to the metal and about froze them in the back seat. It didn't take long to unload our chev passengers. Froze them out. Most of the time we had our old buddies along and looking for a good time. Good old days and fun.

Later on, I worked at the Ford garage and Bob worked with Dad at Ney Chevy of Nelsonville, Bob got the 1941 car from me. We worked in the town of Nelsonville and lived on Adams Street with all three of us having cars and so did dad and mother. We paid our board to mother every week and she cooked for us and kept our clothes done up. Including Rona and Dad, everyone lived under one roof so to speak then. We had low-paying jobs and the better-paying Columbus jobs were more money, but with all that driving and paying Flo and Uncle Pete all that board up in Columbus, we weren't clearing much. We moved back to Nelsonville to lower wages and lived with our mother and dad. See when we all moved back up to old Laurel Run from Ryan's Farm down in Athens County and I got a job at Natco Tile Plant we still had this old Desoto and I had a bad wreck up in Haydenville one winter night and got out of my turn off and this salesman tried to pass me on a double yellow line after dark and totaled his new Dodge up and only bent my back bumper. It was like hitting a tank back then.

Anyways Bob got his driver's license and his first car from someone over in Carbon Hill. It was a 1937 Chevy and was pretty worn out but we worked on it along with Harvey Wend who was head mechanic at Ney Chevy of Nelsonville, he knew the old Chevy and could make them run and sound real good. After he got done cussing every car he worked on and would finish he would step back and listen to it run and say now that's a good running motor. He was cussing at it all the time he was working on it. We would do us boy's cars cheap and make them run good "Old Harvey" We all had cars then. Denny, Rudy, Jim, Bob, and all of our friends around Laurel Run and Haydenville made it kinda like an ant hill of cars going in all directions. Brother Bob had a girlfriend who lived in the town of Chauncey near Athens and the Ryan's Farm where we lived. She told Bob that her class was going to the Old Mans Cave by a school bus that would use Route #33 and pass Uncle Ronald's Sohio station. She wanted him to watch for her bus to come by on the way back to Chauncey. Bob told her to sit in the back seat and he would catch up and follow it back to Chauncey. Here came the bus and Bob and one of our buddies were with him when he started spinning out after the school bus and got up behind it waving at his girlfriend June Hammond. They were speeding along on Route #33 behind the bus and near Diamond when Bob Old 37 Chevy's tie rod steering came off. He had no control of the front wheels at all and slammed the metal highway safety fence then went back across to the other side of the road and hit that fence before he came to a stop. I bet June wondered what in the world happened to Bob who was right up on the back of her school bus. It doesn't pay to sometimes show off.

One Saturday or Sunday afternoon, I may have told this earlier in the story, we all were at Walker Track and watched races and we all stopped at Uncle Ronald's Sohio station. I had my date Lois Tigner along with me and I think Bob had Joan Brown with him and Jim had someone with him. We wanted to race on up Laurel Run to our home at the time and on that dusty gravel road. We had a long stretch between Laurence Wolfe's home and the Old Bennett Farm where Ed and Nellie White lived so all three drivers had our foot to the metal so to speak. There were 3 cars running fender to fender on a narrow gravel road and we were banging running boards together and a one-lane bridge was coming up fast. I was on the far left side with Lois beside me and we had the top down when the soft shoulders of the road started to pull me over to the cornfield. It made me have to let off the gas and I forgot who made it across the one-lane bridge. We all slowed down like good little boys with our girlfriends and also on a nice Sunday ride with Mother and Dad sitting on the front porch glad to see their three boys pull in.

When Jim, Bob, and I were living down on the Ryan farm I was out of school and trying to find a job around Athens because of the drive and gas, along came the big rains. The old Hocking River was coming out of its banks and it flooded all of Uncle Wiley's and Aunt Ivalou's corn fields over the village of Chauncey was a low area that flooded out when the river was overflowing. Everyone would move their things upstairs and the river ran right through their homes and they all had boats to paddle in and out. What a mess it made for cleanup. Well, we boys would take off the fan belts on our old spoked-wheeled car and we set up higher than most newer cars. They would drown their motors out trying to splash on through and they set and we could pass them by going and coming. We were having fun until the state patrol made us stop and go home. We would put our fan belt back on and go Our merry way.

Here's another story for the readers

I was down around the plains and into Chauncey one hot summer evening looking things over and I had this nice looking 41 Chevy convertible with the top down. It got late and dark on me and back then most cars had 12 and six-volt generators on the cars to help charge up the batteries. I had the 41 all lighted up like a Christmas tree and my motor would keep stopping on me and I would turn off my running lights and I was running on what battery I had left to keep it going but wouldn't carry both. I was at a parking lot near Paul Shibes bar and my plan was to be ready to tail someone's car into Nelsonville to get help to get home up in Laurel Run. I got my Chevy convertible ready to go and here comes a car out of Chauncey on old Route 33 and I thought I'd follow his tail lights into Nelsonville about 7-8 miles from where I was. By the time I went through my gears, they never knew I was in back of them while they were flying and I could only see their tail lights fading away. I must have been running at 90 miles an hour in the black of night and I was in trouble. I also knew no one coming at me would think here comes a young man running almost 100 m.p.h. in the dark but I could see Nelsonville city lights in the sky and it was around 12 midnight. The set of the other cars was gone out of site and I got to Harry's Gulf station at the end of Nelsonville, parked on his lot, and called someone to come and pick me up until morning. God was watching over me that night and I knew the highway's long straights anyways. I was lucky I didn't meet two cars coming at me.

When we had moved out of the small house at Ryan farm I was the tractor driver on Grandpa's co-op. The tractor which was a fast road tractor and had a 6-cylinder motor would really get it going even back then. Man, was it cold that one morning when I was pulling two, David Bradley, Rubber Tired, wagons, and Grandpa Doodle and Dad were driving our old model A Ford. They were already half drunk when we left Laurel Run with me pulling the two big wagons. I was dressed warmly with a ski mask pulled down over my face and when

113

I went on to start loading here came Dad and his dad falling around not really doing anything to help me out. I loaded everything on those big wagons and off for Laurel Run and the Wiggins place I went. On the way from the Ryan farm, I was cold and when I reached route 33 I opened the co-op up and man would that big tractor run in the road gear and the smoke stack was blowing out black smoke. Both wagons came along behind me and a state trooper pulled up alongside me and then back off behind me. I don't think he ever saw a tractor move along as I was doing. Household belongings tied on. Pretty soon he went on by me and when I was passing the Vinton Club there set our Old Ford and no dad and grandpa in sight. I pulled the wagons from Chauncey's farm to Laurel's run in 45 minutes. I had helped to unload our household belongings. I don't know when Dad ever got back.

We three boys always had car stories to tell about our first cars and so on and I had gotten my license in 1946, a few years ahead of Bob and Jim. They went with me a lot of the time as a group. They helped buy gas for any trip we were on along with our buddies also. We never knew where we were to end up with so many areas like Logan, Nelsonville, Athens, Carbon Hill, Starr, Coonville, Conneaut, Lake Hope, Old Mans Cave, Ash Cave, and Conkle Hollow. We would go around McArther and to Wellston then to Jackson and Middleport along the Ohio River or down at Luke Shoot Dam and Stockport Dam. Head on up to Rokeby Locks and to McConnelsville around the locks, you may find us anyplace anytime. What we did would've driven Dad and Mother nuts if they knew.

Lost some uncles to lung disease. Silicosis, Natco Tile factory, the Diamond factory, and the tie-in with the passing of family members.

We had really lost three uncles to the sand dust like Harold, Ronald, Charley, and other friends I knew and worked with. My double cousin Denny Campbell worked where I did and he worked mostly on the draw gang and got paid on the tonnage that he handled each day and made good wages. It helped break him down while he was young and did the same with Uncle Paul and others in the family who

114

worked on the set gang or draw gang. I think Uncle Paul worked after his tour in the Second World War and was an inspector who had a small hammer and would peck or tap on each tile coming on the belt. If the tile had a different sound that one was marked as a 2nd and some were taken to the dump or scrap pile. Everything had a salt glaze that was made by salt smoke and that was my job. I would bring the heat up by the days or hours to well over 2000 degrees heat then close the smoke stack and go around to each firebox and put so many shovels of salt and calcium in them. While smoke was settling all over each tile it would put the salt glaze on them. I would look after 2-3 kilns each shift, handle about 9 tons of coal per shift and each kiln had a meter on the wall of the smoker house to switch to everyone that was baking tiles for me to watch. We had a chart to tell us firemen how much heat to add per shift and talk about how hot, it was over 2000 degrees inside, and had peepholes in poor to look at spikes that would bend over when they were done. It was white hot and bright to look inside the kilns. Then you start bringing the heat down little by little to cool off the baked tile and to not crack it. It takes a few days before the door gets knocked down and the draw gang is ready to unload the kiln. The heat after the doors on the kilns broke down came out with the help of the big air fans blowing the heat out. I don't see how the people on the draw gang, ran a conveyor belt in the building with the bricks or tiles still hot. They could unload the whole kiln by early noon and the day's work would be finished. Now let me tell you readers it was hard work and sometimes short hours but the set and draw gang were real men in those days. There would be wagons and yard tractors going everywhere to the railroad cars to be reshipped by rail and also stockpile a lot of tile for later use. Back then in Haydenville Natco Tiles' sister plant, The Diamond was a large tile and brick factory in the area because up Red Row Hollow was a clay mine. The clay had to be dug out of the mines like coal, then mixed with water and other things to make mix for tile and brick. Uncle Gerald Vollumer was the motor operator to haul on the electric tracks and so was Dusty Reider a good friend of the Campbell family. Digging and loading chunks of clay was just like coal miners did in the mines and nothing but hard labor. I knew Jessie VanBibber and he was unreal as a clay loader who worked and loaded tons of chunks of clay for the factory. He had a daughter, Mary, in my school grade room. Every time you see Jessie he is white from the dust of clay and he lives over on his dad's farm off of Laurel Run. At the time, at Stire's cottages, they said he was a real workhorse. My uncle Ronald Campbell took over the Sohio gas station at the end of Laurel Run Road and at Route #33 and we all had a lot of good times at this Sohio station. Uncle Ronald and I put a ball field down in an old basin just behind the station and I was on Ronald's Natco Tile Factory Ball Team. I was 17 years old and at the time when Aunt Waverlene and Uncle Ronald had personal things and needed a break from being at the Sohio station, I would run the place for them. Uncle had trouble with his lungs and breathing from the sand dust in them from working at Natco Tile Plant. I also lost two more uncles to what they called silicoses where the sand dust would just lay on your lungs and eat them away until you couldn't get air at all. Their names were Uncle Harold who died at age 27 and next was Uncle Charley, Aunt Mildred's husband, and Uncle Ronald. Uncle Ronald was taken to Arizona by his wife Waverlene and their two children Larry and Kay my first cousins, when he first was having trouble with his lungs. I was sent back to Ohio after being discharged from the Marines and went to Grandma Campbell's (Brown) home and I got to see my uncle for the last time in 1954. I was home for good from the Marines and got to pay him my respects along with my wife Lois and our baby Denise Rose Huddy. His lungs were being eaten and it was pitiful to try to help him gasp for air. They all moved to Arizona because of the climate there but later moved back to grandma's and that is where he passed away. Our aunt Flo Taylor used to keep in touch with Larry and Kay who are still out in Arizona and keep them up to date with the family and to keep up with their lives. When Aunt Flo passed away they got in touch with me and after that happened we have been keeping in touch with each other ever since. We had a lot of good times with Uncle Ronald and he liked all of us boys the Huddys, Campbells, Vollumers, and all that married into the large Campbell family. You should have seen how many of us were at our family reunion, man, having good talks and reminiscing along with the food. A lot of other hometown men died from silicoses and World War II at that time. One by one our Aunts and Uncles passed on and man so many of our original family are gone and only a few Campbells are still around. Grandma and Grandpa Herbert had Charles, Ronald, James, Paul, and Foster, and the girls were my mother Nellie, Vesper, and Flo and I think they lost two small babies. It was a pretty good size family back then. There are a few of us children still around and up in age and they are two cousins, Dawn and Ray Vollumer, Sonny Campbell, me and Bob Huddy, Rudy and Chuck Campbell, Patty Campbell Dilahay, and Kay and Larry Campbell. The list of the ones that have passed on are Grandpa Herbert and Grandma Nettie, Charles and Mildred Campbell, my mother Nellie, and my dad Thomas Huddy. Gerald Vollumer and Vesper, Margaret, and Ralph, Pete Taylor and my cousin Denny, Zoeta and Cy Lanning, and my sister Rona Lonberger and Gail Lonberger. Also passed are Ronald and Aunt Waverlene Campbell, Paul and Nellie Mae and Patty's husband George Dilahay, and my brother Jim and his wife Nancy Huddy. Brother Bob's wife Joan. This is all I can think of at this time and it is sad and I miss them all.

Uncle Ronald and the Sohio station

Uncle Ronald, his wife, and children Kay and Larry left the Haydenville business of a soda fountain shake shop near the Haydenville Tile Company store and took a stab at the Sohio gas station at Laurel Run and Route #33, and what fun we had there. Man. Ronald got in two or three pinball machines and we would take off the back of it and run or rack up a lot of replays and have free games to last all day. We would feed our faces with ice cream and chips and pop. Two nights in the summertime Uncle Ronald would hire Bob Row's father who showed outside old movies on a large white sheet we hung from two trees near the station and it was free to all. Man, the pop, chips, and ice cream that was sold would cover Mr. Row for the movies and plus. We mostly all had old cars and we got our gas at Uncle Ronald's Sohio Station and he would let us have gas credit until the next payday. My own charge was for around $40.00 per week and at that time I was a kiln fireman up at the brick plant making $1.21 an hour 7 days a week and driving the old 1931 Desoto back and forth to work. I had mostly night work from 11 pm to 9 am and sometimes I wish that I had rested more during the day, it was so hard to stay awake but I would. The next day I would say to myself Man, I'm not going to run around all day and not be ready for my all-night shift, and turn around and do the same thing over again. We had ball games along with the movies at Uncle Ronald's. Everyone was there and Flo and Pete Taylor came down from Logan farm along with Madge and Uncle Gerald Vollumer's family from up in Hungry Hollow. Back in Haydenville with Dona and Ray our 1s cousins, it was more like a reunion to us all. We, dad and mother, lived about 500 yards down #33 along the highway and we had this old car and the state troopers kept an eye on us Huddy boys and at times made it rough on us when we were out for a test drive. On this one hot summer's eve we three, Bob, Jim, and I were out to test driving or something and we were on our way to the Sohio station to get something. At the time our Uncle Ronald was sitting leaning back on his chair under the overhanging roof on the front of the station while I was coming up #33 to turn into the station and a state trooper was heading out of Laurel Run Rd. I turned into the station a little past him and he made a U-turn. Uncle Ronald told me he was coming after us because we had a headlight out and it was near dark so I turned my light switch back to low beams and when he pulled in and came over to the car I was out standing alongside of it. The trooper said, "Son you have a headlight out". Old smarty me went to the front of the car and looked at my lights and said, "No they are both on and burning" and he looked and said to me "alright wise guy lets turn on your bright lights" and wouldn't you know it, it was out and he said to me " Mr. Tom Huddy" and he had my driver's license in his hand "this is the third time I have pulled you over in this old car this week isn't it". I said "Yes" and he asked, "Then wise guy have you ever heard the old saying 3rd time the charm"? And I said yes to that and he continued saying "Now Mr. Tom Huddy your charm just ran out" and wrote me up a ticket and 48 hours to put in a new bulb. My uncle Ronald never let me forget that time. Me trying to get over on that state trooper as he was taking in every word, the state was reading the act to me. The trooper told me if he pulled me over again he would have to take the old car off the highway and asked "Know what I mean"? And added, "I'll be watching for you son". Every once in a while, Uncle Ronald would ask me to look after the station when he had something to do or wasn't feeling well from the silicoses. I helped out sometimes by pumping gas, washing windshields, and so on. My Uncle Ronald was a real cut-up around us teenage boys and with all the fun things and treats there was a real hang out for us boys.'

Susan Huddy Blais

Strip mining company

The Todd Farm was sold to a strip-mining company from up around great lakes and our dad worked for them as a laborer and a shooter of dynamite man and we boys would walk out to help fill up paper bags called dummies with fine dirt. Then a big auger drilled between the dirt and on top of the coal and helped push a 10-pound stick of dynamite, called red diamond, back into the drilled hole. The hole maybe went for 100 feet or so and then with big long tamping poles, the blasting caps, wires back, and tamp in with the filled paper sacks we helped fill. I would get a headache when handling the nitroglycerin 10-pound sticks and it hurts so bad when it gets in the bloodstream. My head pounded like someone hitting it with their fists. After we had tons of 10-pound tubes of TNT shoved back in the deep holes Dad would take a lead wire from the box plunger and tie each hole to a lead wire and everyone got under cover. Dad and I took the box of plungers with the pushdown handle and went way back from the high wall where the TNT was tamped in. The caps would spark off when Dad would push the handle down and they called fire in the hole by everyone in the stripping area. The whole earth just came up and fell apart with smoke and it sounded like a big thunder in a storm. Man. Then dozer and big scoop bucket tractors would push loose dirt off the top of the coal and get ready for drillers to drill down in the coal and shoot smaller sticks of TNT in every hole. Those would be shot off and broken up into smaller pieces and then the shovels would load the loose coal on coal trucks one after another hauling it away to washers. We watched everything as their machines, how they uncovered coal by taking off tons of dirt to get to it and it was called back then strip mining. We three Huddy boys watched the big shovels moving dirt and coal along with the bulldozers and big gear movers of all kinds. We would be up on a high ridge and play around and not go around the sinkholes or quicksand they were called because they would suck down anything that fell in them and they were bottomless. Everyone warned us not to go around them at all and we knew where they all were man. Now the old farmhouse was where buddy Harold, and his brother Don lived. Harold was my age and then Don was in Bob's class and James I think was in brother Jim's class we all played together in the summertime because they were all about our same ages. They had moved away from that place when the farm was sold to the mining company to strip. Truckloads of TNT were put in that old house in wooden boxes and crates to keep it dry and to be near the stripping area and companies got away back then with things like that. If that farm ever went off, man it would blow the whole country and Nelsonville away and it only had no trespassing signs at the end of the mud road. Everyone in that area would stay away from the old TNT storage farmhouse except we boys who would go there to pick purple grapes and to get drinks from the old spring of good water after the Todds moved out. On this same farm were the whole hills of the Todd's Hollow I hunted in for squirrels and there was a thicket of Laurel bushes with green leaves on them year around and they had small like white berries on them. There was also something called a holey tree that also stayed green year around and this was why the road or hollow was called Laurel Run road. We would cut some Laurel bushes in the wintertime around Christmas and holidays and use them for decorations and greenery. That hillside was full of snakes in the summertime like copperheads, rattlesnakes, and a lot of black snakes so the only time we ever went in the brushy hillside was in the dead of winter when every bush and thing was frozen stiff. Now later on in years we three young men deer hunted on the old Todd farm and the old strip-mining area and also rabbit hunted near the old barns that were nearly fallen down with age. Our school friends the Todd boys and their dad and mother moved to our place at the crossroads in the old John Thompson place and rode a different school bus than us Huddys did. We did go out and play with them and had a good time with them. Their father was Grenny Todd and he and his brother were home builder carpenters and they were fast and good.

121

Susan Huddy Blais

Ted Grove family

Ted Grove's place was just a small road passed Tommy Cook's driveway and about 1/2 mile was their farm and home and they went to our Union Furnace school. The oldest boy Jim was my age and Jerry was Bob's age and they had sisters named Jane and Sue. We had a great time also with them, Jim and Jerry were on our 4-H softball team and their father Ted was a gas and oil well pumper and drove everywhere to keep wells pumping. Their mother was a schoolteacher.

1946 and we were in our teens

We moved from our little house on Route 33 in the year 1946 to go to our Uncle and Aunt Ryan's farm that Uncle Wylie got and paid for when he lost his leg on the railroad while changing coal cars at a small railroad yard named Corning, near Athens Ohio. He got a settlement so his dad and his dad's brother owned this large farm with a lot of river bottom land and some hillside farmland together. We were well up in age, Jim the youngest was 13 by now. Our Uncle lived in a small house up above the big farm before the accident. The older Ryans after they sold to my uncle moved to Athens and retired because of old age. Uncle Wylie and Aunt Iva Lou Ryan had five children and Uncle Wylie worked at Natco Tile and Brick company along with our dad Tom Huddy. Around 1946 Dad was sick with his stomach troubles and couldn't work to keep us three boys, Rona and mother so Uncle Wylie let us move up in the small house above his big farm, which was near Chauncey and the City of Athens. That small house was empty after they moved into the farm. They remodeled the big farmhouse and put out a lot of money to restore it and Dad helped work on it when he felt like working and wasn't sick. Aunt Iva Lou was my dad Tom's sister so too helped us out in our hard times we lived on the farm rent-free and our Uncle gave us a milk cow. I milked every day and they helped us out with other foods like eggs and meat. I was out of school at that time and young in age and couldn't get any work so I worked on the farm and helped in that way so we could make it while dad was sick. Rona was home also and brother Bob and brother Jim went to Chauncey school along with the Ryan children. I also hunted a lot and brought in many rabbits, quail, and wild I game to help and drove the old car to church and Sunday school every Sunday all the way up to the Church of God where we went for years at Laurel Run. The winter of 1946 or 47 was a mean one so right in the winter Dad and Mother decided to move back up to Laurel Run Hill into the old Wiggen's farm next to Grandpa Dow Huddy's place. Grandpa Dow helped us out and I took two rubber-tired wagons and went down to Uncle Wylie's farm on a cold winter day and loaded the wagons up and pulled all of our belongings in the two wagons with Rrandpa's co-op tractor up Route 33 to our new place to live on Laurel Run Hill. I walked every working day up to Haydenville, Natco tile plant to try to get a job and stand around with other boys and men on a job. It was 7-8 miles each way for me to walk and they would come out each day and hire 2 or 3 men for work and tell the rest of us sorry men that is all we need today. I would walk back home and do this for more than 3 or 4 weeks. I got home one spring day kinda low because I couldn't land a job, I had turned 17 that winter before we moved back to Laurel Run and I had made all the trips to Haydenville to try to get a job. Well, that morning I had just gotten home and Mother and Rona were at a friendly lady's home to have a party like every week all the ladies who lived up Laurel Run Road visited someone's home. A car pulled into our driveway and a 6-foot redheaded man honked his horn. I went out to see what he wanted and he got out of his car and asked if Tom Huddy was around, I said he wasn't here at the time and he said to me I'm looking for young Tom Huddy. I told him I was and he asked if I wanted a job over at Natco Company and I said "Sure do". His name was Red Brooker and he needed 4 kiln firemen tomorrow morning. I was so happy I said I would be there at 7:00 AM and so that day they hired 3 other young men and me to fire the kilns. Red told me he would be my boss's foreman firing kilns. I was tickled to hear they also hired three of my long-time friends and buddies named Page Martin, Jim Moore, and Ralph Walker. I also worked on other jobs and I remember one 8-hour shift I shoveled 16 tons of course salt into a building and made the old timers mad at me because they said to me it's enough for two shifts to handle like 16 hours and I made them look bad. I had to watch and learn. My first day I was so hot firing all the coal, 9 tons, and in between the hot kilns working hard and no air and each kiln had 200 degrees heat in them plus 90-95 degrees out from the hot summer day. When I got home my dad asked me how I made it today and I said I don't know if I can handle it or not Dad. He said just hang on and you will pick up know-how every day and it will help you out, son. I worked at Natco Tile and Brick for almost two years, mostly night shifts, by then Mother and Dad sold the little house on Route 33 close to Campbell Lane where Grandma's home was and got a nice house down on Adams Street and I met my friend Till Pollack who was from Athens and going to Ohio University and that's when he and I one day were having our lunch and he told me to get away from that place and find an easier and better-paying job. He said do it and get away from here! I stopped working firing kilns and stayed with Pete and Flo for a bit and within two weeks we loaded up an old car and headed for Columbus to find better jobs. It was Rona, my sister, my brother Bob, Rudy Campbell, my uncle Pete, and my aunt Flo. We all ended up living in a trailer court and Aunt Flo worked at a larger department store called Lazar's up on a high street in downtown Columbus. With Aunt Flo's pull for us, we were hired. I worked in the warehouse and they worked on the high street in the big store on the third floor. I had an easy job making $1.24 per hour and I never did from that day on miss the old Tile and Brick job at Haydenville and I can thank my friend Till Pollack for waking me up. Uncle Paul and Aunt Nellie Mae lived in the same trailer court as us and Uncle Paul worked there in the white hall on the main street in Columbus at the Cousins and Fern store about 3 or 4 blocks from the trailer court where he lived. Uncle Pete worked at a machine shop across the street from the trailer court. All he had to do was walk across the street to his job. Uncle Paul and Nellie Mae helped out on the big farm that Pete and Flo owned outside Logan Ohio when they decided that country farming wasn't what they wanted to do so Paul and Pete made two 30-foot house trailers in a big barn and had room to make them look real nice. Then they sold the farm and took off to Columbus to look for work and put the two trailers in the White Hall Trailer Court where us three boys and Rona stayed and got our new jobs. We were crowded so Rudy, Bob, and Rona rented an apartment up near the campus of Ohio State on Dennison and Fifth Ave. We went home in good old Nelsonville every weekend to see Dad, Mother, Jim, and friends.

Uncle Ronald's Sohio station

Here are a few things we were involved in when teenagers and young.

We all had gas credit at our Uncle Ronald's Sohio station which was at the end of Laurel Run Road next to Route 33 and if we turned right we would go toward Nelsonville or turn left and go to Haydenville and Logan whichever we chose. On the way to Nelsonville, we passed our small home on Route 33 and Campbell Lane and along a stretch of highway and then a curve and there was brick plant no 2 Natco Company where my brother Bob worked with my uncles Dow Huddy, Foster Campbell and Willis Gaston all of them worked there at that time and the row of company houses were slowly being tore down because it was an old brick town and not many houses still stood. The grocery store where Dad and Mother had a charge account when we used to row downriver to get pop and food for our campsites was there. OK, back when we were teenagers and not a care in the world to hamper us three, it was just good times. There was a small airplane runway across from the railroad tracks where brother Jim, almost took a plane ride that took the lives of a few of his pals. The plane went down up near Logan and Jim didn't go along with them that night as he had been. Just our God keeping him back. The railroad was called the Hocking Valley Railroad which ran along the highway and route 33 and next to the Hocking River where we had our camps. The same railroad that the early morning freight train tooted at us boys about 1 or 2 O'clock when we were camping in our teens. We had so much fun and good times. Brother Jim may not told you of most of his youth and stories like this so I'm letting you know a few things that I have saved up in my memory store. I must tell you Susan to share them with someone else coming along later. I hope someday some latecomers may want to know some of the things I saw while in my younger days. We three Huddy Brothers would hit Nelsonville with a big bang and man what a good time we would have with some of our old schoolmates, pals, and buddies because we lived in Nelsonville two times and I played football for them when I was a 10th grader and went back to Union Furnace High School and to do that I lived with my aunt Mildred and Uncle Charley and family until I quit and went to work in 1948.

In 1950

In the year 1950 around Thanksgiving Day of that year, we had around 24 inches of snow and I went to work in Columbus when I, Rona, Bob, and Rudy Campbell rented and boarded with Uncle Pete and Aunt Flo Taylor. Ohio was covered up with that big one and I got the last street bus on the high street going my way toward our home in The White Hall Trailer Court and Main Street that day. The driver of that bus told me this is as far as this thing is going to take us friend and all-electric pole buses were parked along the curb and had taken down their trolley electric poles maybe so other buses could get by. I stepped off in the deep snow up to my belt and walked right down the middle of Main Street in the city of Bexley and walked around two miles home. Back then only 4-wheel trucks were old World War II trucks and jeeps and only a few of them were owned by different gas stations. The snowstorm was on a Saturday when Ohio State played Michigan in what you may have seen called the Blizzard Bowl and they still show old newsreels on sports channels. I worked that day and man was it snowing hard and no way could I get out of the parking lot so that stopped all work at the warehouse. A large delivery truck with chains on the tires took us all over to big department stores on the high street to try to catch a street bus or try to find a way home. Anyways we four young ones wanted to go to our own parents' home as we did every weekend and have fun with Mother, Dad, Jim, and all of our buddies and take in some movies in Nelsonville or Logan. It broke our hearts that Route 33 to Lancaster Logan was all closed because of the bad snowy weather. We had to spend that weekend with our Aunt and Uncle and wait until another week to get to Mother and Dad's. It was the deepest snow I have seen in my 80 years here in Ohio.

1950-1951 Girlfriends and fast driving

Eventually, Rona, Rudy, Bob, and I moved back to Hocking Valley and we had our girlfriends Lois and Joan to date about every night. We decided to take turns in our cars and drive to Columbus every day and we did and kept our jobs in Columbus but tired. We stayed out late and got to bed and Mother would get us up around 5 o'clock in the morning and take turns driving to work. If the driver got too sleepy we would change drivers with one another while the other one slept. Brother Jim was still at home with his mother and dad so was Rona. Bob and I would say to each other, Man I'm going to get some rest tonight I'm asleep on my feet and don't you know we would do the same thing over again knowing we needed rest. That's the part of being young. Anyway, we had to keep our sweet hearts happy that was our future wives and both went to the same school Buchtel York High near Nelsonville. Lois and Joan's school buddies didn't care much for the Huddy brothers including Jim who was 4 years or so younger than me. Because we invaded some of their girls from under their noses but we all three had our own cars and what were the Buchtel School friends going to do about it anyways? The year was 1950-1951 so that is why we moved back to Athens and Hocking Valley and drove to our work up in old Columbus Ohio. We were well known for miles around large cities and small towns when they knew the three Huddy Boys were near. Because we had a lot of buddies that hung around us from all over far and near. Us three would park side by side on the square and you would think there was a big fight going on with all the girls and boys around us on a Saturday evening everyone wanted to get in on the fun and the city police didn't care much for us three and would keep an eye on us by cruising by in police car and wanting to arrest us for but we outsmarted them a lot because they knew our dad and came and told mother and dad to keep a better watch on us three because we were breaking laws in Nelsonville and dad asked him what all we were doing by breaking the city laws? They said "Well, Mr. Huddy your sons speed everywhere they go in town and run stop signs, spin or burn out, leave tire marks on the streets, and have loud pipes and muffler exhausts and all kinds of wolf horns and ship fog horns and house door bells and all lite up with lights and hood angels are on the nose anything to draw attention and draw a crowd you name it and they have done it. You better talk to them Mr. Huddy and Dad said "he would find out what we were doing in Nelsonville and about the complaints coming from the law". At the dinner table, Dad had us all together and brought it up to us about the police coming by and talking to him. Dad said, "What is going on with you boys behind mothers and my backs"? We said "Well Dad nothing much at all but they don't have anything to do but pick on us and try to drum things up on us. We're just having fun with boys and girls we know" and that was about all that was said by Dad and Mother. They told us to try to hold it down some. We had a good time we three brothers and drove fast and hard, everyone knew our cars on the gravel road up Laurel Run, and man, the dust was bad and I bet they who lived below our home would say I wish these Huddy brothers would slow down and not stir up so much dust. All good people and most had sons who ran with us. We all got along well knowing each other's families and all of us went to school when we were younger on the same bus route. We had our buddies most all had cars or hot rods and on Saturday evenings we all went to Nelsonville and we all had our rides looking real nice following each other around the square. It was show-off car night and always a lot of boys and girls around us when we parked all in good fun. I spent the whole day Saturday cleaning and waxing my car so it was shiny and clean. I did even the side walls so there was nothing out of place so it would look good driving around the square and meet all of our buddies and see what's new on their cars. We usually had the same bunch in town on Saturday night like Rudy, Denny Campbell, and all three of us Huddy boys Tom, Bob, Jim, and other friends from far and near Logan, Haydenville, Red Row, and Union Furnace, Carbon Hill, Carbon Dale and some from up at Pattonville and even Chauncey, the Plains from all around and from the countryside all far and near all mostly smart show-offs. All of us had illegal exhausts and all kinds of whistles, bells, wolf and fog horns. We had weird sounds and all kinds of lights, mud flaps, curb finders, all colors of birds and angels on the front of the hood, some extended continental wheels and rear everything to draw others' attention as we went by. We or most of us met in a restaurant called Busy Bee and we'd have an after-midnight snack before we headed for home and rest and sleep to recharge for the next day. When I dated Lois and Bob dated Joan it slowed to a different pace. Brother Jim had a girlfriend also.

I was 18 at the time and didn't meet Lois until 1951. I was waiting to be drafted by our service into the Korean War so we stayed with Uncle Pete and Aunt Flo until we quit our jobs and went back down home to stay. We were not long in Hocking Valley when Bob and I came back to Columbus and got a job at the machine shop where our Uncle Pete worked and we both drove from Hocking County for a year back and forth 5 days a week. At home where we all lived, we, three boys. Jim, Bob, and I, had cars and hot rods and kept the roads hot. I went to work at the Ford garage in Nelsonville and Jim went to work at a greenhouse nursery store also in the town. Our dad and Bob worked jobs at the Ney Chevrolet garage in Nelsonville. Dad and Mother owned a nice house on Adams Street and Rona stayed home and helped Mother with the cooking and home care. Bob, Jim, and I paid board to Mom and Dad to keep home life going.

Uncle Pete and Aunt Flo

I want to tell a bit about Uncle Pete and Aunt Flo and all the good times. We all loved them and the things those two did to show us all a great time. Uncle Pete fit right in with us all from the start. We boys loved to see him and Flo show up at our place. They always had a little something for us to wear in whatever the season was at that time. I remember one cold winter when Dad was out of work and we were having it hard, Uncle Pete and Aunt Flo came to our home with new winter coats, nice. Flo worried about us, I heard on her way from our place she cried her eyes out so to speak because of our hardships. I remember on Christmas we lived up on Grover Hill Street in Nelsonville and Dad was working so to speak and along came Flo and Uncle Pete and had new gloves and scarves and nice caps for us boys to help in the wintertime. We loved them so much both of them always had new plans and new things to do and would take us up to their home or farm and we would help them with it and maybe keep us sometimes 2 weeks at a time and show us a good time. They would take us fishing and hunting for everything even pigeons. Flo was a good cook and would make us squab on toast and we would clean fish catch and Flo and Pete's sister Alice would fry them. They would even take out small bones for us and we would pick wild strawberries with Flo's homemade shortcake and cold cow's milk, man what can I more say? At that time they lived in Fargo near Marengo Ohio and had milk cows, all Russ had an old model A Ford and let me drive we boys everywhere. Always showed us a good time. We didn't want to go home at times. Russ was Pete's sister Alice's husband and they loved us boys. Russ was in the Marine Corps. in the 2nd World War and was hurt in house-to-house combat, shot in the neck which almost killed him. He would take us boys to any place to fish around the area like small creeks that you could jump across in some places and catch bluegills, bass, catfish, and almost any freshwater fish in the creek. This one creek ran across many of the big farms plus Russ would take us over to Alum Creek a bigger one to fish anytime. Then Flo and Pete got a farm in Thornville and tried to raise beef cattle and farm some hay and plant corn for livestock, we boys helped out a lot in the summertime. While on summer vacation, Pete and Flo would take us over to Buckeye Lake to the park and ride the roller coaster, go on boat rides, fish on some of the islands, and take us to drive in movies and the works. We always dreaded going back to the old grind that Dad had ready for us. A list of work to catch up on as long as your arm. Then Uncle Pete and Aunt Flo moved to a farm near Lake Logan and we all helped them move. They had a lot of cows and we helped milk them each day to send it to Logan Pure Milk Co. Then lost most of the milk cows with a disease called Bangs and no longer could they sell the milk and it broke up their dairy farming along with all the farming back then. We helped them farm and our families got together a lot for good times and ball games. I had the old DeSoto and my driver's license at that time and we went to Pete's to help harvest crops and on or after a hot day in the hay field we would drive to Hocking River with soap and wash rags and towels and bathe in the river. It felt so good and then to go back to Logan farm. Aunt Flo would have a nice meal ready for us. We all had so much fun around Pete and Flo no wonder that we wanted to stay with them. Uncle Paul and Aunt Nellie Mae moved in with them in the big farmhouse and they, Pete and Paul, built homemade house trailers to live in and they were planning on leaving the farm and going to Columbus to work. They sold out and made themselves two nice trailers to live in and moved to White Hall Court in Columbus. Then Mother and Dad moved to the town of Nelsonville on Adams Street and I went to work at Ford Garage, Bob to work at Nye Chevrolet, and Jim at Whitmore's Nursery and Garden Shop. Rona stayed home with Mother and Dad worked with Brother Bob at Nye Chevrolet garage. This is where I decided to go in the Marine Corp and get it over so I enlisted in January 1952. Now you have noticed I haven't said much about my uncle James Campbell who lived up around Waynesburg Ohio in the Canton Area and Massillon. We lived a ways from them and only saw them at reunions so Jim and Pete and Pete's wife and Patty their daughter came to visit. Patty was a lot of fun for a cousin and she maybe would stay for a week or two at our grandma Campbell's home and we would run around together and have teenage fun in our old car. She sometimes had a cousin from Logan who came with her named Gene Ann Pierson also Uncle Jim put in big shaft vault doors for banks and vaults to make bank money safe from bank bandits I guess for safekeeping or so. I really didn't know much about my Uncle James. My Uncle Harold Campbell died at the age of 27 and his son Sonny was my cousin, his Mother was Avenell Smith from Carbon Hill, which is a few miles from Haydenville and Nelsonville a small town so again I think I was in 5th grade when he passed on but I remember him. We had some fun with Sonny and used to shoot frogs and play in the creek that ran near Grandma's place. I played basketball against Sonny in our high school team in Hocking County and we played each other and he was a good player. I think my story covers most of my uncles and families so I only know as much as I was told or heard for myself or what I lived while growing up. On the Campbell side mothers, brothers, sisters, and husbands when you come from a large family like we did you sometimes have to ask who are those children and whom they belong to.

Marriages, services, families, and family history

Bob was dating Joan Brown from Buchtel York High School, her father who was an insurance man around Nelsonville and had passed on and her mother Willa raised Joan, Berry, Buck (Neal), and younger sister Karen. They went to school with township children where my girlfriend Lois Tigner lived but went to the same school as Buchtel High. At that time brother Jim had a lot of girls he liked and dated but never knew only if he came by Dad's and Mother's house or if we saw him out on the road or in town. He stayed at home with His Mother and Dad for most of his younger years until he went into the Army. When we would ask Dad, "Where is Jim, "? He would say "I don't know Tom he jumped in a carload of girls 2 days ago and where he went I don't know". Maybe he stayed where ever and came home a week later. It was hard to keep in touch with him because Bob, Rona, and I were married and only saw him some weekends at home. He kept the roads hot so to speak and ran fast every place he went. I got brother Bob to follow me into the Marine Corp. and I'll tell you of some of those days later in this story. We told Jim of boot camp in the Marines and he was going to enlist and I think we said too much of what the Marines had to do and he changed his mind and took the Army instead. That's OK we all were serving Uncle Sam's armed forces that's what counts. Jim ended up on the East Coast and went in the Army training and Bob and I went to the West Coast for our boot camp training. Lois and I were the first married out of our family. I came home on a 20-day leave and we were married on Fort Street, at the Church of Christ in July 1952. After our wedding, we all went to Dad's and Mother's for a family gathering, and sister Rona did a lot of work along with Mother to celebrate our marriage. Plus, we had a party for our marriage and a going away party out on the Old Bennett Farm near the fire tower on Zion Ridge. Man, what a turnout for us. Lois and I went in Bert Tolliver's car to make a trip around the square with a just married sign, honking horns and dragging cans behind us. Now on the way from Nelsonville to Zion Ridge Farm was called Lick Run Hill and there was a long steep hill. We went up Lick Run Road going along at a decent speed when here came a Chevy car like the wind speeding around us all and blowing its horn. Guess who it was but one of us Huddy boys, Jim. Bert Tolliver said "Can you believe someone running that way on this road and driving that way, man he is crazy," then he asked, "Do you know him"? And we both, Lois and I said "Yes", it's my youngest brother Jim". If I remember correctly Ruth Ann was with him at the time. He was at home with the motor cooled off before we got there. Bert said, "I can't believe anyone in their right mind would drive that way on that road". We had around 200 hundred people at that party and you should see the gifts. I believe we got around $100.00 cash which helped at home and on our trip to California which was 2,600 miles away. It came in handy for us. Our service buddy and wife lived in Bellefontaine Ohio and I'm not sure if it was them or us who had a 1948 Chevy and we drove it both ways from California and Ohio. Bob and Chester Wood took us up to Bellefontaine to catch our ride. Lois and I had our new lives together away from all our families and had a great time in Oceanside California and my Marine Corp. days. She was really homesick for a short time but after a while, she was okay and started to enjoy California and her new married life with me. We got a lot of mail and phone calls back home in Ohio from our families. Our first home was with a Marine buddy and his wife and their little girl. He was saddest to his wife and we rented a trailer our first real home together. It was in the same court that the Henrys lived in. Later we rented a nice trailer on Route 101 coming into the ocean side and lived there for a year then we got a nice apartment that the Marine Corp. owned and we rented that at the edge of the ocean side for only $27.00 per month. We managed okay until I was sent overseas to Japan and I had to send Lois home to wait for me to get my Marine Corp over with and she was going to have Denise without me. Lois went back and lived with her mother and dad until I got home and sadly I was in Japan when Denise was born. It took our troops ship 17 days to get us to Japan and I was there for 9 months. On my way home, I passed Bob's ship and he was going to Korea at the same time I was on my way back home. I had a lot of fun in Japan putting in my last few months in the corp. I went to a big gym and played basketball, lifted barbells and weights, and boxed with gloves and that is when I spared with a light heavyweight of the world 3 rounds. He was from the country of Jamaica and was 190 pounds and I was around 210 but I gave him all he wanted in the 3 rounds and had him in the ropes. In those 3 rounds, he was a boxer and me a slugger, I'd been in boxing ever since my high school days and at home with about everyone who wanted to put gloves on but mostly with brother Bob, who was my main sparring partner, right, Bob? We two had a lot of scraps in our hay day, playing ball games and always lined up on sides against each other. When we left Japan, I landed in San Francisco California on December 8, 1953, and had to stay at Treasure Island out in the bay which was a Navy base until January 8, 1954, and got mustard out to go home. I flew home to see Lois and our baby Denise Rose for the first time when she was 3 and 1/2 months old. Lois and I went back to Nelsonville so I could go to my old job at the Ford Garage because the old job waited on me to get out of service. Now Jim was still at home at Mother's and Dad's place and Bob was still over in Korea when Lois and I moved to Columbus to work at a job there. When Bob got home he and Joan got married in Nelsonville and went to live in Buchtel a small town near Nelsonville from Athens County. Rona had gotten married to Mr. Gail Lonberger from over around Murry City and was in Athens County too. Gail worked on the railroad and that was up in around Columbus so that is what the Huddy family and Lonbergers were doing in those days. Lois and Denise lived up in the city of Columbus, Rona in Columbus, and Jim at home and with mother and dad until he also went into the Army. Jim met Nancy while stationed on the east coast and they got married in Massachusetts and then she came home with him. By then I went from my job at a machine shop on Main Street and was in White Hall called Ortlepp and Spohn, which was a German family-owned. Then Lois and Denise moved up into the north end of Columbus and I got a job working for Columbus Coated Fabrics making plastics and wall text, wallpaper, Samsonite luggage covering, oilcloth, and other things. It was a big factory, blocks long, and on Grant and 5th Ave in Columbus. I worked for better than 15 years there and Lois and I lived down near the Children's Hospital on Gilbert Street where Joe was born. At that time Bob was in the small town of Brice Ohio that was just outside of Columbus and worked at a paper-making factory in the South end of Columbus for a few years. He then went to Hawesville, KY to work for a bigger paper mill on the Ohio River across from tell-city Indiana. At that time Lois and I also had our youngest son Glen. Bob and Joan raised their family there and most of them are still living around that same town until this day. Bob and Joan had 5 children together named Vicky, Laurie, Becky, David, and Matt and they are all married and with their own families now. Joan Brown Huddy passed away, our sister Rona and her husband Gail passed, and our mother Nellie and our Father Tom also went to their graves. Our brother, Bob, after around 3 years remarried a Kentucky girl named Jackie and we love her so. I hear from my brother Bob now and then and he kept me informed about our brother Jim, his wife Nancy, and their two children Kevin and Susan who had all moved to Maine. Kevin their son and oldest stayed living in Maine and Susan their daughter moved to Florida as did Jim and Nancy later on in life. Then the news came of Jim's wife Nancy passing away and that he was very ill. One year and 5 months after Nancy passed Jim passed away as well. Susan and her husband Phil cared for them both while they were ill in their home except for Jim's last 7 months here on earth. Brother Jim and Nancy hoped to celebrate their 50th anniversary together after they learned of Nancy's bad health and they were able to a few months before Nancy passed away. Now there are only the two Huddy brothers left from the original family of 6 Huddy's. Brother Bob and I are in our seventies but we have our children and grandchildren to carry on after us and the Huddy name. We have a lot of good memories of growing up in our family in the hard times and the good times. Lois and I have been married for 58 years now. She is not well and I care for her with the help of our Church, some very kind folks, and a care organization. We are all praying for God to lift her up here in the City of Newark, Ohio where we live at home and also near to our three children and their families. Denise and her son Kip live near us and Joe and his children, Joey, Courtney, and Tommy do too, and our son Glenn and Tina live within an hour's drive. A lot of the Campbells, Huddy's, Vollumers, and Ryan's, and also a lot of our cousins have passed away. A few notes here that popped up in my old head. Patty my cousin from up in Waynesburg, Ohio wrote a few lines of her and her dad my uncle James a while back in my book story. When I came back on the ship from the Korean War, her husband was a Marine named George Dilahay. At the time, I didn't know him but we came back to the USA on the same ship and I met him later on. It is such a small world and now he is passed on and I really liked him.

My life and the moves Lois and I made

I have been in landscaping for years and years and that takes in the digging of trees and planting flowers and shrubs and sodding, seeding, and got even to Africa to landscape a long way from here took 29 hours to get there to Nairobi Africa and I stayed for 2 weeks to landscape for our Church of God everything paid by our own church a great experience to me. Also, Lois and I raised our children up at a farm between Jackson Town and Hebron Ohio on the Old 40 route near Buckeye Lake. They went to the Lake Wood school. Then Lois and I moved around a bit like from Columbus and out to Avondale on Buckeye Lake and then to Sunny Acres at the town of Hebron and the town of Buckeye Lake then out to Uncle Pete's and Aunt Flo's boat landing and then we got an acre of land in Jackson Town and put a large 14X70 expand there and later sold that and moved out by Thornville on Ridgenour road where Pete and Flo had a farm back in those days. Then we moved to Hebron and then over here to Newark on Jefferson Street. That is where Lois had her first stroke and I had 3 stints put in my arteries for my heart. God has been good to us and let us live still and then we moved here on Channel Street and Maple here in Newark, Ohio and we have been here for better than 10 years. I am able to help take care of Lois who is down with diabetes and 2 strokes that weakened her terribly. All I can say is thank you God for letting us live. July 31 we've been married 58 years and our oldest child Denise is 57 years old, Joe is 53 and Glenn is 50. Like I said, "God has been so good to us." Down through my younger married years, I loved my sports. Hunting, fishing, and racing, and had my 1" old Model A Ford as my vehicle now I have had nearly 200 cars in my time and I love older cars and like to go see them here on the square and at the big State Fair in Columbus where some 6,000 cars are to be seen. You can look at them until your eyes get sore, haha. I would love to own and restore an old car but it takes a lot of time and money to do it. I have a 1958 Fairlane four-door 500 Ford. I have had it for a good 10 years and I'm having a hard time finding parts for it so before I ever get it finished I will die of old age. I remember when Bob lived in Brice he got a 1957 6-cylinder Chevy that ran well for a 6-cylinder. I took it down to Sugar Grove to run against Brother-in-law Eldon Wolfe who had a new 1960 6-cylinder Chevy and blew his doors off. Dad and I think I had Bob's Chevy up to 108 mph at the top end. That's good for a 6 cylinder. I had a 1958 Ford stick shift with a 312 Thunderbird V-8 and I could get it up passed 125 mph and was always putting in new transmissions. I raced everything on the road like Plymouth, and Chevy products and a lot of 57 V8 Chevy and I had a Ford mechanic work on it all the time and he had it running good for me. His name was Carl Harold and he was all Ford and his brothers Wayne and Ed Roush were all Chevy. Wayne was always bragging about his 57 Chevy that did run well out here at Hyde Park and had some good speed times. Kept telling his Ford brother that he could blow Tom Huddy's Ford doors off so we were ready for him and Ed Roush his Chevy buddy after work off to old sawmill road to run it off. His brother was with me and told me he was tired of Wayne's bragging and mouth and wanted me to help do it and Carl had been working on mine right along. Off of the starting line we had both lanes open for miles, and no one came toward us so I knew my Ford in low or 13 gear was a real quick car. I had him by a car length in low range and when we hit 2nd his Chevy came back on me and by then we were somewhere between 90 and 100 mph and open roads. I had a 3-car lead at 125 mph and old Wayne said Tom that's the fastest Ford I ever raced on the streets. He had a lot of respect for my car. Another time I was going home to Gilbert Street and on 3rd Street at 5th Avenue knew I hadn't had my car too long and 2 black boys pulled up beside me in a black new Plymouth Fury and looked over at my Ford and asked "Hey man will that gray 58 Ford run"? I said "It's not too shabby" and they said, "Let's run one off here". I was all for it and had my motor already half opened up and riding my clutch and when the light turned green that Ford jumped out to a 3 Car lead and here they came with an excuse of getting stuck shifting from low to second and we stopped at the next light and I said "Let's run it again" and away we went and they really tried to run that Plymouth Fury with me and we stop again and they said to me "hey man that Ford had been worked on to run like that pull over down here someplace and let us see your power plant and I said "some other time guys". I traded it off later and let a boy at Columbus Coated Fabrics take over my credit union payments and I also took his 1953 6-cylinder red and black Chevy that brother Jim wanted so bad and he had an Olds 88 he got from Rudy Campbell and I wanted more getaway speed. I traded Jim cars and no sooner had we traded than the trannie went out of mine and I was back to square one on cars again. I think at one time I had over a dozen cars and trucks on Stygler Road in Gahanna, Ohio. I was all the time car and truck dealing. I had a 1931 Model A Ford I was restoring in the garage. I always loved them. My buddy at Coated Fabrics had another Fairlane 500 from off Ohio turnpike and had a 152 hp motor in it and a high-range rear axle, I got it from the credit union and he lost his job and they took it back now it was all dressed up with a continental wheel on the rear, black, red and white interior, that big engine under the hood. At the top-end speed, I really didn't know how fast it would go after I had it up to 130 mph and everything got real cute and at that speed, I shut it down. I was heading for Buckeye Lake on the new freeway out of Reynoldsburg just looking for a good race in the afternoon and here it came up behind me, an all-black 1958 Chevy Impala and a young boy out to show it off by blowing by others. I was watching him move up on me and I was still in second gear and he swung out around me and I let that horse go, man, it surprised him, so he floored the Chevy 58 V8 and the race was on. We were flying side by side at 130 mph and Cy Lanning was going to work, on the other side of the freeway and saw us coming near Kirkersville and he said "The wind from us almost blew his car off the road. I got an old 1939 Buick Coupe from my pal at Coated Fabrics, it had a straight 8-cylinder in it all chromed up, and had 8 carburetors one for every cylinder, and a big electric fuel pump feeding gas to every cylinder and they said, "It was made to run a flying mile". Up at the old airport that was shut down they made a drag strip of the runways and told Ed when he got it that it clocked at 120 mph in a flying mile where you had a running start at a mile and timed your speed. How true this was I didn't know and I sold the motor to brother Bob and he put it in a 1937 Ford Coupe. I think it was front-end heavy. I don't remember what he had done with it at the time he and Joan lived at Buckeye Lake Trailer Court. Those were our speeding days and we went to Columbus Motor Speedway and up to Powell Ohio, to Hyde Park Drags and also state fairgrounds and our own race track at Pattonville also at Guysville. We love also tractors and 4X4 truck pulls so we had the bug and we even had go-karts and anything that would run or race. I made a race car that I got from up around a car row man who worked with Bob and me named Les Ruble, he had a 1937 Ford and I had Cub Ackerson haul it down to Laurel Run and paint on the side P-38 after the World War II fastest airplane. Mother and Dad wouldn't sign for me to race it up at Walker Race Track so I gave up the idea. I would have to be 21 years old or have my parents sign for me. I was only 18 at that time. An old German lived next to where Bob, Uncle Pete, and I worked in the Whitehall Machine Shop and he wanted us to look at some old cars that were covered with tarps under a mulberry tree. There was also a homemade midget racer so he showed us a Rollsroash with big high-spoke wire wheels, an 8-cylinder engine, and a big luggage box on the rear. There were spare tires in both front fenders and we asked him what he wanted for it and he said "$35.00". At that time, we turned it down and today it would be worth 35,000.00. Wasn't looking down the road very far. I paid him I think $15.00 for the quarter midget and got it home at Grandpa Huddy's place and couldn't get it to fire or start so with brother Jim watching me and Bob driving in his 37 Chevy they were pulling me. We went down across Hocking River bridge and I told Jim to watch my hand signals and tell Bob to slow down in case it started. Jim was in the back seat looking down on me because Bob couldn't see me that low and close to his car. I gave Brother Jim a slow-down signal and Bob wasn't reading him right and running fast to try to get the racer to fire and Bob just slammed on the brakes of his car thinking it was a stop signal I gave. I only had a one-wheel brake and I went all the way up under Bob's car to my steering wheel, caved in my hood and windshield, and pinned me in my seat. I was mad at Bob for going so fast but he thought it may start at a higher rate of speed. That was the end of that small race car. All smashed in. Everywhere we 3 Huddy boys went it was like going to a fire or the law was after us even if we went over to Route 33 to Sohio for a soda pop. We dusted everyone's house who lived beside Laurel Run Road. We never gave it a thought until my older age set in. Sorry everyone for our actions. Our friend Millard Patton loved us boys and loved sports and made basketball courts so we could play on nice ones. He had a small Willey's Coupe and it was his pride car and was as clean a car you'd ever seen anywhere around. One Sunday morning Millard was in the services inside of the building when we boys wired a smoke bomb to his spark plugs. When the motor was turned over to start the smoke bomb would whistle and then go off and talk about smoke. Old Millard came out of services and we all knew what was coming, he started it up and the smoke bomb did go off and we thought he was having a heart attack right then. He jumped out and raised his hood to see if his motor had caught on fire because he had never seen a smoke bomb or heard one scream. I think for the first time he was mad at us boys, or embarrassed in front of the older saints coming out to get in their own cars. You should have seen the show. One morning or noon we boys and our friends on a hot Sunday morning, were walking home and Mother and Rona got a ride with someone else. We boys while on the walk home played a long way around the river, got under the bridge, and took off our Sunday school clothes to go skinny dipping in the river. Red Walter Baumgardner had his good Sunday, Church suit on and was out in the river in our row boat and told us he didn't want to swim. That was a big mistake on his part and we upset him out in the middle of the river, shoes, suit and all. He went on up Laurel Run Rd cussing us and crying saying Mom and Dad will kill me. Walter was our fall guy and always had to be in trouble in some way. A good pal and was a schoolmate of brothers Jim and Rudy and wanted to be with us all the time like others also. We had a good bunch of boys our ages around us and that's when Chuck Wood, Chet's dad helped start 4-H there in the hollow of Laurel Run. We all got along pretty well with each other and not too much fist-fighting. Most of the fights were between Bob and me while the rest of our buddies sat down and waited for the fight to finish so we could all go back to playing our games of basketball or football. They would be yelling at us to stop fighting and play ball. Now if I ever would admit it I started a lot of the fist cuffs on purpose because I knew he couldn't control his temper. He was faster on foot speed than I was and could out-jump me on the basketball banking board so I made sure on my way up or down I gave him a good lick inside with my sharp elbow. I knew he would lose it after a while and start throwing punches and haymakers. He's the only one of the gang who wasn't afraid of me and stood toe to toe and dished it out. He would get all steamed up and say you see what that cotton picker is doing on every play and I'm fed up with it and his temper got the best of him. I knew when he was ready to start swinging. I love him and always did and liked to get him mad just to fight. Bob, I was good for a high school boxer and whipped every boy in my weight and size and a lot of them just thought they were good until they came from other small villages to challenge me. We always had gloves around because we had our school gloves at home most of the time and Bob was the only one who would spar with me. He would hang right in there, man. Chet Wood was my age and a little bigger and taller than I was and his dad Chuck was telling me how Chet his son could whip almost everyone in the 4-H and around Haydenville. Bob said "he can't whip Tom" and Chuck said "I bet he can", so the fight was on. On went the gloves and Chet was left-handed and I knew he was afraid of me. His dad was cheering him on and Bob and Jim were backing me up. Chet I knew really wanted to run but he would take a round swing house left to my head and I hit his jaw every time and spun him around like a top. After 2 or

3 rounds he said "That's all for him" and his big mouth dad said "I thought you were better than that Chet. Then I took on older boys like Denny Bill Evans, Gene Sparks, Loyd Schull, and boys from Haydenville and Nelsonville. I also took on Louis Vernon and his brother Bill who was 2 or 3 years older than I. When I was in the Marine Corp. and about 210 pounds I used gloves a lot over in Japan and boxed a lot of tough men. The lightweight champion of the world, 190 pounds from Jamaica wanted to fight someone and came by our gym to practice with volunteers for his upcoming fight. His manager asked me to spar with him for at least 3 rounds and I wanted to do that just to prove if I was good at it or give it up. I had the first 3 rounds with him and I knew what he had in mind. He came on like a wild stallion and I gave him some ground to try and figure him out. He every so often dropped his gloves like to say come on and that was his mistake and I put on my fury and had him in trouble and into the ropes. In the second round, he was a real storm and rushed me with everything he had and was outpointing me with a lot of punches. In the 3rd round and last round, I let him use up a lot of fuel, and man I set into him with barnyard slugging and he fell into the ropes and was hurt with his nose bleeding. I had him glassy-eyed and really hanging on and after the fight, his manager came over to me and asked "Marine do you have a manager"? I said, "No, I do this for fun" and he said, "Get one you're a good fighter". I had a lot of practice with Brother Bob. On the way over to Japan in August 1953, I was lying down in the D department about 40 feet below the top of the water and I had just written a letter home to Lois and my buddies came running into our area in the D department and said, "come to topside Tom this Marine has pinned every sailor and army man that came up against him". I asked "What about me?" to my buddies and they knew I liked that tough wrestling and boxing so they talked me into going up on deck and a large crowd of servicemen were there watching the matches. This Marine was named Elwood and was from North Dakota state and I would say about 240 pounds and a tall, lanky, all-solid boy. I was someplace around 225 or so and I've had a

lot of fights in both wrestling and boxing and this guy named Elwood said, "Hey Huddy want to try your luck like at the Fairway at Ohio State Fair?" That kinda got under my skin and I said "sure nothing else to do but sail on to Japan." They had a big taped-off circle on the still deck and it was a free for with no getting on your hands and knees to let the man get a hold of you. It was just barnyard rules and into it, we went, he was taller than I was so I went for his neck and I clamped on to it like a crab and cranked down on it and had all 225 pounds pulling on his neck and right off there was his weakness, his neck. Man, I went to work on it time and time and he tried to pick me up to get me off my feet but I had that hammerlock on his neck and the catch was mine with over a thousand men watching us go at it on the deck of the troop transport the U.S. Howe's. That made me a lot of new friends also. Bob if you're reading this story remember you and I could take the 50-pound scale weight and pump it 70-80 times and some of our pals had to take both hands to get it up one time. When I got out of the Marines at the age of 22 I could pick up 100 pounds in my teeth and jaws and stand up and hold it for a while now I don't have any teeth only store-bought teeth, haha. Buchtel Town is where Joan and Lois went to high school, later called Buchtel York High, and is still that today but now a new highway passes the city of Nelsonville altogether and goes by Buchtel Town past the old trash dump in Nelsonville, to Old Twin Lakes, down at Old Dorr Run and in behind the brick town of Diamond. It runs passed the old Bud Wolfe place and connects to four lanes at old Red Row Route 33 near our old clay mine and cemetery. I guess Nelsonville is out of the traffic and all the business is over around Buchtel I heard but haven't seen it yet. I hear say but I'll get down that way one of these days now. The old country is changing a lot and old Laurel Run Road is all black top now a big change from way back when. Our old home of logs at the crossroads burned down and it looks so different now. As the wheels of time turn, so does our past. Anyways everything passed by us and I wonder sometimes who's all still alive we knew while growing up. I know some of our old gang, I call them, are gone like

Chet Wood, Walter Baumgardner, Ralph and Gene Sparks, and cousins Denny Campbell, Rona, Gail, Ronda Lynn, and Zoeta, and others we knew. Our Aunt Mildred and Char, Uncle Pete and Aunt Flo, Aunt Ivalou and Uncle Wiley, Ryan, Shirley, Barb, and brother to them Jack my age so little by little we are thinning out. That's the way our God planned it. Also, Steve Huddy, Pauline and Uncle Dow Huddy, Uncle Jim and Lena Huddy, Foster and Margarete Campbell, Linda, Ronny and Sue Campbell, Shorty and Denny, a twin. On and on our old loved ones have gone on. We are the old ones now we are up in years and are the old ones now. I think, Ray and Don Vollumer are the oldest and then me at 80. Not intended for us to be here forever. It's what God gave us a short time here. Like my sweet Grandma, Campbell Brown told me one time sitting in a chair in her yard after putting two of her sons away and I asked her how she felt about her nearly outliving all her children. She told me ", Tommy God gave them to me to enjoy for as long as I did and now they are a dream story to me". She was a very good wise woman. The life she led and told all of us children about serving the Lord God while growing up under her good heart and watchful eyes. I'll never forget her along with my mother and all my aunts and Mildred's family having family prayer in her house. She was the piano player also. I also helped her when her son Paul was a prisoner of war overseas and I would help her pack a 10-pound care package for him until he was freed to come home. I have seen that all while growing up near her. She was of the Mounts family and I knew them all and used to go to her Brother Kelly Mount's home for a get-together with their children who also went to school at Union Furnace. I don't think I ever saw Grandma Campbell mad and she always was a pleasant saint to be around. I would drive her to deliver her boxes of Christmas cards to Red Row, Wolfe Basin, and Haydenville at Christmastime. In the spring I helped her plant her garden and cut grass for her. She loved to have her grandchildren around her a lot and to pick berries. I think of my mother Nellie Edda when she was bitten by a copper head and if it wasn't for Grandma Campbell her mother sucking out the snake poison from her leg when she was a young girl, my mother Nellie would've lost her leg. A lot of good stories about Grandma Campbell. Grandma married Herbert Campbell from up in Haydenville and at the end of Campbell Lane were Nellie and Harvey Wend and Nellie was Grandpa's sister also from Haydenville. Grandpa Herbert had two or three brothers I knew of, one was Arley, and one named Flave who used to live in Chet Six's place years ago and lived next door to Ott Evans a lot of uncommon names back then it seems. Anyway, old Flave had a pair of snow-white doves that coed a lot and had them in a big, big cage and they were so beautiful and loved one another it seemed very much. My Grandpa Herbert and Grandma built the old Campbell home when they first married and had a large family of children, he was a factory worker and later on, worked on that highway road construction until he died when I was in about 5th grade.

Boys and their wives			Girls and their husbands		
Charley-	Mildred	Huddy	Vesper-	Gerald	Vollumer
Harold-	Avanell	Smith	Nellie-	Thomas	Huddy
Ronald-	Waverlene	Martin	Flo-	Pete	Taylor
Paul-	Nellie Mae	Pearson			
James-	Peat	Pearson			
Foster-	Margret	forgot?			

One more child passed away when I was a child and I do not remember its name.

Anyway, most people had large families back then and that's almost everyone I can recall knowing. Then along came us children like a storm from everywhere and place. Don Vollumer was the oldest of the grandchildren down to the youngest, and what a gang of us in all at our Campbell reunions. Now only a handful of us original ones are still around so to speak. Some have moved away to other states and some are still within an hour's drive from my home in Newark. Ohio near Buckeye Lake where Aunt Flo and Uncle Pete had the boat and fishing marina years ago. Lois and I have one girl Denise and two sons Joe and Glenn all within an hour's drive from us here. Our children all went to Lakewood High School near Hebron, Ohio, and Buckeye Lake so we raised them on a farm near Hebron and near Jackson Town next to the school on Old National Road Route 40. Good children and so are their children. Joe had three, Denise two, Glenn none, and Lois and I loved them all and also our grandchildren and great-grandchildren. Watching them grow from year to year makes me feel younger, haha. Lois, as I told earlier in my story book is almost bed fast now and I'm starting to get help from the state human services to send someone to help me here with Lois and help me out.

Tom Lee Huddy

Tom Lee Huddy was 78 years of age at the time he started writing his notes and approximately 3 years later.

Part 1 is finished in May of 2011.

Edited and typed by Tom Lee Huddy and Susan Huddy Blais

Nelsonville, Ohio
early 1900's
grandpa Dow L. Huddy

Rona Huddy
Tom Huddy Jr.
Bob Huddy
Way back when.

Jim   Bob   Tom

1940's

Jim   Bob   Tom

Tom and Nellie Huddy
1964

1924

Tom   Nellie

Dad
Thomas Huddy

Mother
Nellie Huddy

James Huddy

Tom Huddy
in front of my barracks

Bob Huddy

Rona Huddy　Tom Huddy　Nellie Huddy
Jim Huddy　　　Bob Huddy　　　Tom Huddy

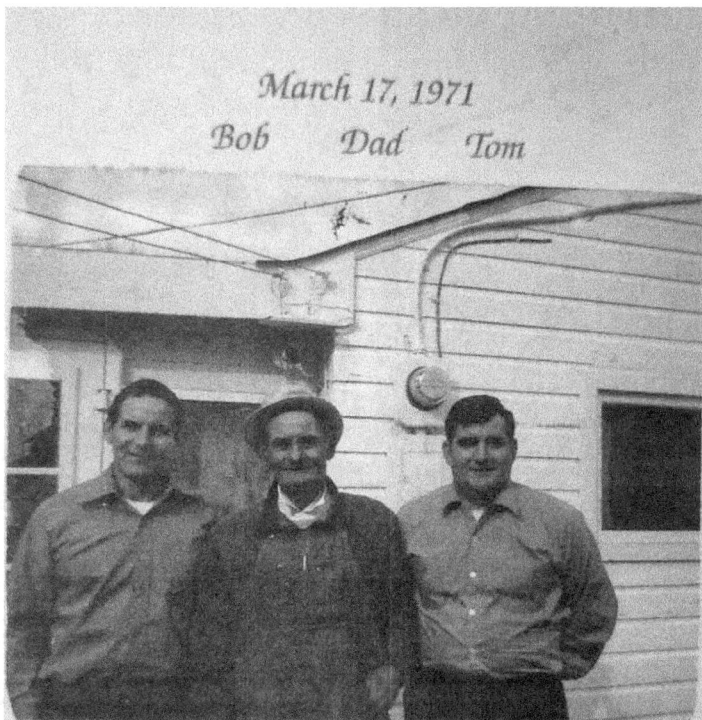

March 17, 1971
Bob   Dad   Tom

Rona Lonberger
"Rona Huddy"

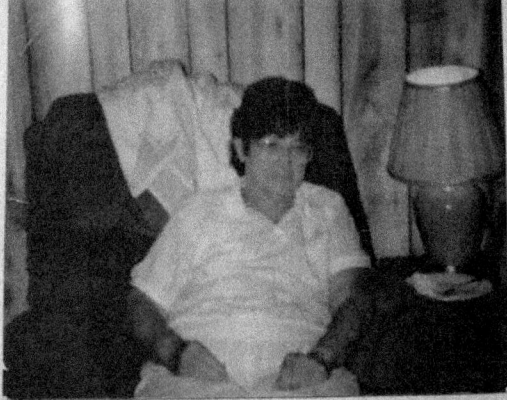

Buchtel Marine Now In Japan

Marine Corporal Tommy Huddy, shipped out of San Diego, Calif. the first of last week for an extended assignment in Japan. Cpl Huddy, son of Mr. and Mrs. Thomas Huddy, Buchtel has been in the Marines 19 months and this is his first foreign assignment. Mrs. Huddy, the former Lois Tignor, has been living in Ocean Side, Calif. with her husband until he was shipped overseas. She flew home on Monday just less than 12 hours from California. She will make her home with her parents at Doanville, until Cpl. Huddy's return. Tommy is due for another promotion in October.

Area Athlet With Marines

CAMP PENDLETON — Two former Columbus-area athletes are now teamed together with the 3d Shore Party Battalion, a unit of the 3d Marine Division at Camp Pendleton, Calif.

Captain William N. Mack and Private Thomas L. Huddy have both played on basketball courts and football fields in and around Columbus, Ohio.

In 1940, Bill Mack was presented the Agonis Award as the outstand-

Buchtel: Tom Huddy Called Home

By WILLA BROWN

The Amos Tignor family, Doanville and the Thos. Huddy family here, were delighted to have a long distance telephone

Daughter Is Born

NELSONVILLE — Mr. and Mrs. Thomas Huddy (Lois Ann Tignor) of Nelsonville, are announcing birth of a daughter, Denise Rose, on Oct.

Susan Huddy Blais was raised in Maine primarily but has moved a total of 32 times since her birth in 1961 to the present day. Self professed tomboy, adventure seeker, and caretaker by trade. She now resides in Maine, after 20 years of living in Florida with her husband Phil, and their two children.

This book came together as an idea Sue had while talking with her Uncle Tom and Aunt Lois Huddy after she contacted them late in their years. Sue hadn't heard much about her father's life, from the 1930s up until he married her mother Nancy. After her parents' passing, she reconnected with her Uncle Tom. He began to share the three brothers lives growing up and she was excited to write their story. He would send her packets of handwritten tales and then later they would talk about them over the phone. Sue was so enlightened as to why she had a wild side growing up and now it was clear. She, indeed, was her father's daughter. This whole book is truly from Uncle Tom's handwritten memories. The hope is that you enjoy stepping back in time as much as she has.

www.ingramcontent.com/pod-product-compliance
Lightning Source LLC
LaVergne TN
LVHW052026080426
835513LV00018B/2192